# yan-kit's classic
# chinese
# COOKBOOK

# yan-kit's classic
# chinese
# COOKBOOK

## Yan-Kit So

LONDON, NEW YORK, MUNICH,
MELBOURNE, DELHI

## To my son, Hugo E. Martin

**Editor** Elizabeth Watson
**Senior Art Editor** Nicola Rodway
**Executive Managing Editor** Adèle Hayward
**Managing Art Editor** Nick Harris
**DTP Designer** Traci Salter

New photography art directed for DK by Carole Ash
New photography by Martin Brigdale

### DK DELHI
**Editorial team** Dipali Singh, Shinjini Chatterjee,
Glenda Fernandes
**Design team** Kavita Dutta, Romi Chakraborty,
Mini Dhawan
**DTP team** Balwant Singh, Pankaj Sharma,
Harish Aggarwal

First published in the United States in 1984
This edition published in 2006
by Dorling Kindersley Publishing Inc.,
375 Hudson St, New York,
New York 10014
A Penguin Company

2  4  6  8  10  9  7  5  3  1

Copyright © 1984, 1998, 2006 Dorling Kindersley
Limited, London
Text copyright © 1984, 1998, 2006 Yan-kit So

A Cataloging-in-Publication record is available from
the Library of Congress

ISBN-10: 0-7566-2351-0
ISBN-13: 978-0-7566-2351-7

Reproduced by Colourscan, Singapore
Printed by Leo Paper Group, China

See our complete catalogue at **www.dk.com**

# Contents

# Foreword

I first met Yan-kit in the early 1980s when we were both demonstrating cooking at Prue Leith's school. She was elegantly dressed under her starched apron, and tiny behind the demonstrating table. She was nervous and talked very fast with a strong Chinese accent. We went out for coffee together when we were finished. She seemed a very unlikely cook or even cookery writer. She was scholarly, with the aristocratic air of the educated Chinese who, although refined gourmets, looked down on cooking as a menial occupation. But she showed an amazing determination to transmit the gastronomic traditions and practical culinary techniques of her homeland. At that time, although Chinese cuisine was generally considered the second-greatest in the world after French cuisine, the Chinese food familiar to Europeans and Americans was on the level of the debased cheap carry-out. Recipe books in Chinese were hopeless, giving little indication of quantities, timings and techniques; and in China, the Cultural Revolution had reviled the grand style as bourgeois and persecuted the great cooks.

It was after the loss of her American husband, Briton Martin Jr., when she was left alone with a tiny baby, that Yan-kit took up cooking with great passion as a salvation from her enormous grief. She wrote several Chinese cookbooks, two of which are among the best on the subject in any language. Yan-kit had very high standards for everything in life; she loved music, opera, poetry, art, and fashion, and she put the great force of her intellect and knowledge, her incredible good taste, and her love of good food into her projects.

*Yan-kit's Classic Chinese Cookbook* was her first book. It was an early bridge between the East and the West and remains one of the best introductions to Chinese cooking. It features recipes from all the regions of China, though it represents more of the delicate cuisines of the east coast, Shanghai, and the area south of her Hong Kong childhood, than the stronger-flavored, cruder cooking of the northern and western regions. The recipes are more refined haute cuisine than basic rural food, but many of the dishes are very easy to prepare. Yan-kit was a purist, eager to keep the recipes authentic, but she made them accessible. She tested them so scrupulously, and described every step so clearly and meticulously, that even the complex recipes are easy to follow. Like many of her friends, I was privileged to eat at her house when she was testing dishes. They were all stunning and utterly delicious. I am so happy that the book has been reprinted in such a glorious production.

Now that China has become the biggest economy in the world, a superpower that we will have increasing contact with, we will need to understand Chinese culture. Food is an important part of that culture. The Chinese are mad about their food. The old grand dishes are being revived for banquets and in the new best restaurants. With Yan-kit's book we can make them our own.

*Claudia Roden*

# Introduction

My interest in food is inherited from my father. Although he did not cook himself, he always asked Mother to see to it that what was on the table was correct, right down to the last detail: for him, stir-fried dishes had to have "wok fragrance," sugar was to be used very sparingly in marinades; chicken was not to be overcooked lest the flesh became tough; fish for steaming was to be bought live from the market and abalone was to be well seasoned with oyster sauce. Like children in other Chinese families, my brothers, sisters and I joined the grown-ups for dinner from the age of four or five, picking with chopsticks from the dishes served in the center of the table. So it isn't surprising that what has stayed in my mind is delicious well-prepared dishes, seasoned to Father's liking, rather than the bland food given to young children in the West.

From those early childhood days in Hong Kong I also remember Father taking us to restaurants where we had delicate hot tidbits, *dim sum*, or to the boat restaurants in Aberdeen for special seafood. Every year, during the month following Chinese New Year, his *Hong* or import-export trading company would give a banquet to which our whole family as well as those who worked for him would go. At these banquets the menu would follow a prescribed procedure: two small, hot seasonal dishes followed by shark's fin, either as a soup or braised in a sauce, next a chicken with crispy red skin to augur another prosperous year, then a duck or perhaps succulent pigeons, followed by another soup—turtle or something else equally exotic—then one or two more stir-fried dishes and lastly a whole steamed fish, the pronunciation of which is the same as the word "surplus," which can signify abundant wealth.

Having taken good food for granted, like so many other Chinese, I did not think seriously about it until I became a frugal postgraduate student at the University of London. Short of cash but nonetheless hungry, haunted by the tastes of both home-cooked and restaurant dishes, I began to try my own hand at cooking Chinese food. To my delight, I found I was adept at it. One dish led to another, and soon I found that I had become an enthusiast, cooking with zest and satisfying not only my own palate but many others'.

This amateurish approach took a marked turn in the early 1970s when I spent a long summer with my young son in Waterford, Connecticut. There I used to entertain my American family and friends with Chinese dishes, and I remember their surprise that the tiny Niantic scallops could be so succulently tender when simply stir-fried; that the Cherrystone clams, delicious served on the half-shell New England style, could make one's mouth water equally, if not more, when cooked in black bean sauce with garlic; and that sea bass and bluefish could be so refreshing steamed with slices of ginger and seasoned with a little soy sauce. They were equally enthusiastic about the strips of pork I roasted, then brushed over with a little honey, and with ox tongue braised slowly in soy sauce and sherry. For my part, I found cooking remedial, relaxing and rewarding. The seed of this book was sown then.

Since that time, I have worked with different Chinese chefs in Hong Kong and London, been to China and Taiwan to sample different regional cuisines, entertained at home, and taught and demonstrated Chinese cookery both privately and publicly. The invaluable reactions of friends and students led to much pondering over food and cookery in general, and Chinese food and cookery in particular. I discovered that many people who are very enthusiastic about Chinese food are, unfortunately, in awe of Chinese cookery. They claim it is time-consuming, fiddly and generally incomprehensible. But since every form of cooking takes a certain amount of time and involves some technique, however trivial, the first two points are irrelevant. On the third point, I strongly believe that Chinese cookery can be as comprehensible as any other, and this book is an expression of that belief. How? First, by taking each recipe and breaking down the method into clear steps, and by giving precise explanation (and in many cases an illustration) of how and why certain methods or techniques are used. Second, by illustrating every recipe to show what the dish should look like, and third, by describing and illustrating any special Chinese ingredients, so that they can be properly selected. Above all, by presenting a fair sample of classic dishes, my aim has been to enable every cook to achieve the desired authentic effect.

# What makes food Chinese

Whatever the arguments about the greatness of Chinese cuisine, it is undeniable that certain features make the food look Chinese, smell Chinese and taste Chinese.

One feature, unique to Chinese cooking, is the technique of stir-frying. A small amount of oil is poured into a heated wok and a few condiments are added to "arouse the wok" and lend fragrance to the main ingredients, which are rapidly stirred and cooked in a short time.

This technique requires specially prepared ingredients. In Chinese cooking these are cut up into uniformly small pieces so that they will both absorb the taste of the seasonings they are marinaded in and retain their freshness, juiciness and crispness.

Another speciality of Chinese cuisine is its use of dried products. Before the invention of canning and deep-freezing, drying was the Chinese way of preserving food. But even though canning has become a Chinese industry and frozen food products are now exported abroad, dried products are still widely used and are very often more expensive than corresponding fresh ones. This is because the dried products, when reconstituted, add an extra

dimension to the taste and richness of the finished dish. For instance, the flavor and fragrance that dried Chinese mushrooms so miraculously lend to other ingredients are beyond the capabilities of fresh mushrooms. The same can also be said of dried scallops, dried oysters, dried shrimp and dried abalone, one of the most exotic ingredients in Chinese cuisine.

Nowhere in other cuisines is there such a pronounced emphasis on texture. Exotic ingredients like shark's fin, bird's nest, edible jellyfish or duck's feet, and everyday ones such as cloud ears, bamboo shoots or cellophane noodles, often have little taste, yet the Chinese go to any amount of trouble preparing them, combining them with other ingredients to lend them taste. Why? Nutrition apart, it is the texture, whether crisp, elastic or slippery, that they provide that makes them invaluable. Emphasis on texture is also apparent at a more basic level: leaf vegetables, whether boiled or stir-fried, must retain their crispness; noodles must be served *al dente*.

Monosodium glutamate (MSG) is a white crystalline substance which adds a meaty sweetness to food. It is used widely in Chinese restaurants, but as some people react badly to it I do not use it in home cooking, nor have I used it in this book.

## What is a typical Chinese meal?

To the Chinese, a meal comprises rice or another grain, with a few dishes. The number of dishes accompanying the rice depends on the number of people sharing the meal, but a family of six may have three or four dishes at dinner, and perhaps one less at lunch. Obviously the more dishes, the more festive and special the occasion. Whatever the number of dishes, they should be well balanced, so that in one meal a variety of ingredients, including meat, seafood and vegetables, is eaten, and different cooking methods appreciated.

## Laying the table

Because a Chinese meal is a communal affair, a round table is usually used, being more conducive to sharing of the dishes. For each place setting you need one rice bowl, a matching saucer and a pair of chopsticks. As the name so aptly suggests, the rice bowl is for the rice, the saucer underneath is for food taken from the communal dishes before you eat it, or for the bones you gently spit out. The chopsticks are placed vertically to the right side of the bowl and saucer—the Chinese do not seem to have made concession to left-handers!

The basic table setting is a rice bowl, saucer and chopsticks. On occasion you may also need a soup spoon and small dish for sauces.

In China it is considered good manners to hold the bowl on your lower lip and to shovel in the rice.

## How to serve a meal

On a day-to-day basis, all the dishes are served together in the center of the table (with extra rice kept warm for second or third helpings). There is no specific order for eating the dishes, so one may have a mouthful of chicken followed by another of bean curd, followed by yet another of fish. However, for more formal occasions, the dishes are served individually. The sequence of order varies from place to place, but generally one or two seasonal "delicacies" are served at the beginning, followed by substantial dishes of meat and poultry, with special soups in the middle and a fish to end the dishes. ("To have fish" is pronounced exactly the same as "surplus," in Mandarin and Cantonese, so the Chinese frequently use this pun and choose fish symbolically to end the main dishes.) Then, one fried rice and often one noodle dish will be served. This is the host saying, with traditional polite modesty, "Excuse my humble fare which may not have been sufficient, so please fill up with some grain food!"

## How to eat rice

The proper way is to raise the bowl with one hand and perch it on your lower lip and then, holding the chopsticks with the other hand, to shovel the rice into your mouth without dropping the grains on the table or floor. Rice symbolizes blessings in life for the Chinese and it is therefore vital for you to grab your blessings in rather than pick away at them.

## Eating other dishes

When you pick up a piece of food from one of the central dishes, it is quite all right to do so at the same time as another person so long as your chopsticks do not end up fighting in the dish. Having picked up a piece, remember to make a gesture of touching the rice in the bowl, however momentarily, before putting the food into your mouth.

When a piece is large in size, whether with or without bone, it is polite to eat it in bites, rather than in one gulp. The bones can be sucked, quietly, before being gently spat out onto the side plate.

The main aim should be to enter into the spirit of the meal and to *enjoy* yourself. Don't forget, however, if you are host, always to put some choice pieces in the bowl or saucer of your guests.

## What to drink with Chinese food

Like table manners, the Chinese are casual about what they drink with their meals. Traditionally, they drank warm rice wine with their food and tea after the meal, but some Chinese have now adopted a habit of drinking beer or cognac or whisky, sometimes straight and sometimes diluted, with the meal. In Chinese restaurants abroad a custom has developed of serving tea throughout the meal. Many Westernized Chinese have also found that some Western table wines, especially white or rosé, go well with Chinese food. Many Chinese never drink anything with their food; they are, on the other hand, more particular about the tea they drink after the meal. There is a wide choice of tea to serve after the meal—jasmine, keemun, Oolong, iron goddess of mercy or Tit-koon-yum, Pu-erh from Yunnan and chrysanthemum, to name but a few. Jasmine is a green tea scented with jasmine petals, originally beloved of the Shanghaiese but now popular throughout China and abroad. Tit-koon-yum from Fukien, gleaming with a dark luster, releases its subtle fragrance slowly after it has been infused in the pot for some minutes. Pu-erh tea is believed to have a slight medicinal property, and is excellent after a meal of rice dishes.

**USING CHOPSTICKS** Perch the chopsticks on the first knuckles of the third and middle fingers so that they lie parallel to each other, resting in the crook of the thumb. Lay the thumb on top of the chopsticks to secure them—the lower chopstick should remain more or less stationary while the upper one is maneuvered by the first and middle fingers in a pincer movement.

# Vegetables

The Chinese love to eat vegetables, and the leafy green vegetables of the *Brassica* family are their special favorites. They boil or stir-fry them, but only for a short time, so that the vegetables retain both their crispness and their vitamins. They frequently use a little meat to enhance the taste of vegetable dishes, and, conversely, use some vegetables in meat dishes to provide an interesting texture.

**Chinese flowering cabbage** This vegetable is usually served stir-fried or simply blanched.

**Mustard green** This variety of mustard green is less bitter than many others, and it is usually served blanched or stir-fried, or in soup.

**Bean sprouts** Tender sprouts of mung beans, used to provide a crunchy texture.

**Sugar peas** Tender, flat green pea pods with barely formed peas. Usually served lightly blanched or stir-fried.

**Chinese celery cabbage** Sweet, mild-flavored cabbage, usually stir-fried or braised.

**Chinese chives** Used to provide flavor, they are stronger than chives, although more fibrous in texture.

**Mustard green** This more pungent variety of mustard green is served pickled or in soup.

**Chinese white cabbage** Although similar in taste to Swiss chard, it is sweeter and juicier.

# Vegetables

As with many Chinese ingredients, texture is important in a vegetable: the spongy hair seaweed is both an absorber of sauce and a provider of texture; water chestnuts and bamboo shoots are pure texture foods. The flesh of winter melon is succulent and subtle, and the slippery taro goes especially well with duck. Ginkgo nuts and baby corn on the cob, often used in vegetarian dishes, add color and variety to a dish. The three preserved vegetables are popular seasonings for meat, soups and other vegetables.

**Chinese water chestnuts** Crisp, sweet-tasting sedge bulbs, used to provide a crunchy texture. They are also ground into flour.

**Winter melon** Green gourd, the flesh of which becomes almost transparent when cooked. It is often used in soup with pork, chicken or duck.

**Taro** Root vegetable, frequently cooked with duck or fatty pork.

**Hair seaweed** Product of Hopeh and Shensi provinces, this rather tasteless ingredient is used to absorb flavor and provide a slippery texture.

**Bamboo shoots** Young shoots of bamboo plants, used for their texture in many Chinese dishes.

**Young corn** Miniature corn on the cob, used in both vegetable and meat dishes.

**Ginkgo nuts** Tender, mild-tasting nuts from the ginkgo tree.

**Red-in-snow** Red-rooted variety of mustard plant that sprouts up through the spring snows.

**Pickled mustard green** Mustard green preserved in brine.

**Szechwan preserved vegetable** Mustard plant preserved in salt, then pickled with chili powder.

# Herbs and Spices

Relatively few herbs and spices are used to produce the sophisticated simplicity of Chinese cuisine. The three indispensable ones are ginger, scallions and garlic, especially for stir-fried dishes. Next in line are star anise, Szechwan peppercorns and cinnamon, all of which enrich the taste of soy sauce-based, slow-cooked dishes. Chilies, especially the dried red ones, are part and parcel of Western Chinese regional cuisine whereas coriander is the beloved of people in the North.

**Garlic** One of the three indispensable ingredients of Chinese cooking, along with ginger and scallions.

**Scallions or spring onions** An essential ingredient in Chinese cuisine. Both green and white parts are used.

**Coriander** Also known as Chinese parsley, it is used as both a garnish and a seasoning.

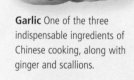

**Shallots** Similar to, but less pungent than onions, they can, however, be used in the same way.

**Mixed spices** Used in flavor-potting. The ready-mixed packages usually contain star anise, Szechwan peppercorns, cinnamon, ginger, fennel, cloves, liquorice and cardamom.

**Five-spice powder** Liquorice-tasting powder used, sparingly, in marinades.

**Ground roasted Szechwan peppercorns** Dry-roasted, then ground, and used to add aroma to other ingredients.

**Szechwan peppercorns** Not spicy hot like peppercorns, the roasted variety produces a slightly numbing effect.

**Chili** Indispensable hot ingredient of Szechwan cooking.

**Sesame seeds, white** White seeds from the sesame plant.

**Star anise** Pungent liquorice-tasting spice used to add flavor to meat and poultry.

Fresh ginger

Dried ginger

Ground ginger

Cinnamon stick

**Ginger** The third essential ingredient in Chinese cooking, used to provide flavor and to counteract any rank odor of other ingredients.

**Cassia bark** Dried bark of an evergreen tree, often confused with cinnamon (above), which can be used as an alternative.

# Cereals, Grains and Noodles

The most important staple for the Chinese, long-grain white rice, is usually eaten with every meal. Noodles are generally of secondary importance, except in the North, where wheat is the main crop and they are eaten just as much as rice. Symbolically rice is blessing in life and noodles are longevity. Not surprisingly, therefore, noodles are always served for a birthday celebration.

**White glutinous rice** Sticky when cooked, this rice is used for both savory and sweet dishes.

**Long-grain rice** The hulled, polished grains of this variety remain the ideal staple for the Chinese.

**Spring roll wrapper** Paper-thin wrapper made from wheat flour and water.

**Wonton wrappers** Made from wheat flour, egg and water and used specifically for wontons.

**River rice noodles** Made from rice ground with water, which is then steamed into thin sheets before being cut.

**Dried rice noodles** White, wiry noodles made from rice flour.

Dried egg noodles, flat

Yi noodles

Dried egg noodles, round

**Egg noodles** Made from wheat flour, egg and water, these are the most commonly used and versatile of Chinese noodles, whether used in their fresh or dried form.

Fresh egg noodles, flat

Dried shrimp noodles

Fresh egg noodles, round

**Tientsin fen pi** Made from mung beans, these are eaten as an alternative between rice noodles and cellophane noodles.

**Buckwheat noodles** Thin noodles made from buckwheat flour mixed with water.

**U-dong noodles** Common to Japan and Korea, these noodles are made from wheat flour and water.

**Cellophane noodles** Eaten more as a vegetable than a pasta, these noodles are made from ground mung beans.

# Dried Products

One cannot get very far with Chinese cooking without dried fungi. They are used, according to variety, to provide texture or taste, and very often make a simple dish outstanding. Black mushrooms, used whole or sliced into small pieces, provide their own taste but also absorb that of others. Both cloud ears and golden needles absorb tastes and are often used to give texture to stir-fried pork or beef dishes; wood ears, which need to be cooked longer, are best in soups.

**Wood ears** Large, edible mushrooms cultivated in large quantities in Western China.

**Chinese mushrooms, dried and reconstituted** These edible tree fungi vary in both quality and price, the most expensive being the floral mushroom. Medium-sized mushrooms are most frequently used in this book.

Floral mushrooms

Straw mushrooms, canned

Straw mushrooms, dried

**Straw mushrooms, dried** Cultivated on rice straw in paddy fields, they are used more for their texture than their taste.

**Cloud ears** Like wood ears, these mushrooms are grown in Western China, but they are more delicate in taste.

**Golden needles** The dried buds of the tiger-lily flower, generally used for their texture.

**Tangerine peel** Dried peel, often used with star anise and Szechwan peppercorns.

**Dried red dates** Sweet, prunelike fruit of the jujube tree.

**Creamed coconut** Concentrated coconut milk in solid form.

**Cornstarch** Fine, white starch extracted from corn, used as a thickener.

**Potato flour** Made from cooked potatoes, this flour produces a more gelatinous sauce than cornstarch.

**Water chestnut flour** Made from ground water chestnuts, and used when a lighter sauce is required.

**Rock sugar** Crystallized cane sugar.

**Agar** Gelatinous thickener derived from seaweed.

# Dried Products

Chinese dried products, used as either the main ingredient
or as a seasoning for more bland ingredients, are regarded
as second to none. Abalone, scallops, oysters and shrimp,
although delicious fresh, are much richer in taste and
more interesting in texture when dried. Bird's nest,
shark's fin and edible jellyfish actually have no fresh
counterpart in Chinese cooking and always have
to be reconstituted before cooking.

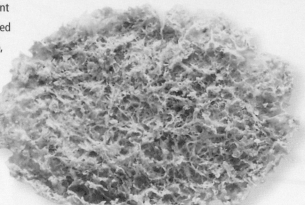

**Bird's nest** Nests of the swallows of the
genus Collocalia, who line their nests with a
thick mixture of predigested seaweed, which
then dries to a hard, transparent layer.

Pork liver

Pork and duck liver

**Chinese sausages**  Wind-dried sausages made of pork
or pork and duck liver. Both should be cooked before use.

**Edible jellyfish** Preserved and dried in salt, the layers must be soaked in frequent changes of water before use.

**Shark's fin** The cured fin of one of several species of shark. Processed fins (right) are more economical to use.

**Abalone** Firmly-fleshed mollusk that is often only available canned. The juice is useful for soups and sauces.

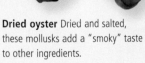

**Dried scallops** Deriving their name from the shell's shape, these mollusks have a deliciously sweet taste.

**Dried oyster** Dried and salted, these mollusks add a "smoky" taste to other ingredients.

**Dried shrimp** Dried shelled shrimp of various sizes, frequently used as a seasoning and in stuffing.

# Beans and Bean Products

Beans and bean products play a prominent role in Chinese cooking, where they are used in much the same way as dairy products are in the West. The soybean, one of the most ancient staples grown in China, is richer in protein than an equivalent weight of any other food. However, because soybeans are hard to digest as beans, they are usually processed into sauces or, more important, into bean curd. Many imitation meat dishes, the backbone of Buddhist vegetarian food, are based on the numerous forms of bean curd. Fermented bean products are very important seasonings in savory cooking, while the red azuki bean, whole or in paste form, is used in many sweet dishes.

**Bean curd, fresh** Made from a mixture of finely ground soybeans and water, bean curd is used extensively in Chinese cookery.

**Bean curd, puffed** Deep-fried pieces of fresh bean curd, used to absorb tastes and juices.

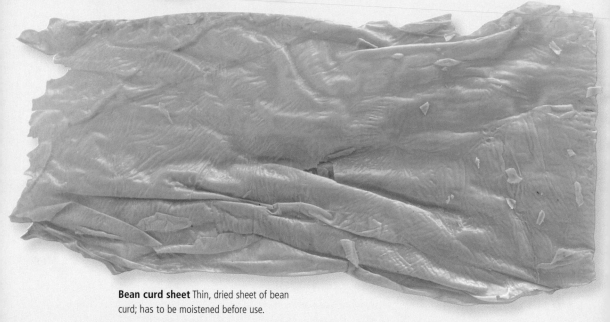

**Bean curd sheet** Thin, dried sheet of bean curd; has to be moistened before use.

**Black beans, fermented** Whole soybeans preserved in salt and ginger.

**Red beans** Highly proteinaceous azuki beans, most commonly used for puddings in Chinese cookery.

**Red bean paste** Thick paste made from puréed, sweetened red beans, frequently used as a sweet filling.

**Bean curd "cheese," red fermented** Fresh bean curd, fermented with salt, and rice wine.

**Bean curd "cheese," white fermented** Fresh bean curd, fermented with or without chili.

**Crushed yellow bean sauce** Purée of fermented yellow soybeans, wheat flour, salt and water.

**Szechwan chili paste** Spicy hot paste of dried chili and crushed yellow bean sauce.

**Soybean paste** Paste of crushed soybeans combined with chili, sugar and salt.

**Yellow beans in salted sauce** Whole yellow soy beans fermented with salt, wheat flour and sugar.

# Sauces, Oils, Fats, Wines and Vinegars

Sauces of various types are used in marinades and to add flavor to cooked ingredients. Soy sauce is the most basic but also the most important seasoning. Used with salt, it helps to turn simple ingredients into Chinese cuisine. Because so many Chinese dishes are stir-fried or deep-fried, oil is obviously an important ingredient, but it is also important for the flavor it gives to marinades.

## SAUCES

Thin soy sauce

Thick soy sauce

**Soy sauce** Made from fermented soybeans with wheat or barley, salt, sugar and yeast.

**Oyster sauce** Made from oyster juice, wheat flour, cornstarch and glutinous rice, salt and sugar.

**Chili sauce** Made from crushed chilies, vinegar, salt and plums.

**Hoisin sauce** Soybeans, wheat flour, salt, sugar, vinegar, garlic, chili and sesame oil combined.

**Sweet bean sauce** Made from crushed yellow bean sauce combined with sugar.

**Shrimp paste** Ground shrimp fermented in brine; available in two strengths.

**Fish sauce** A combination of fish, salt and water.

**Sesame paste** Pulverized sesame seeds. Tahini should not be used instead.

## OILS

**Corn oil** A polyunsaturated oil from corn.

**Sesame oil** Dark, aromatic oil from roasted sesame seeds.

**Peanut oil** Rich, monounsaturated oil with a nutty flavor.

## FATS

**Hot chili oil** Oil in which red chili flakes have been steeped.

**Chicken fat** Chicken fat rendered by slow frying.

**Lard** Rendered pork fat.

## WINES AND VINEGARS

**Kao-liang liqueur** Very strong spirit made from sorghum.

**Moutai wine** Distinctive spirit made from wheat and sorghum.

**Shaohsing wine** Popular wine made from fermented glutinous rice and yeast.

**Mei-kuei-lu wine** Made from Kao-liang spirit and rose petals.

**Chinkiang vinegar** Thick fragrant liquid with low vinegar content.

**Red vinegar** Low vinegar content; frequently used as a dip.

**Rice vinegar** Used for cooking and pickling vegetables.

# The Wok

A wok fitted with a lid is an essential cooking utensil, because it is suitable for all methods of Chinese cooking, especially stir-frying. Woks come in different sizes, for family use, a 14-inch (36-centimeter) one made of carbon steel is ideal.

**Wok brush** Stiff wooden brush used for cleaning the wok after use.

**The wok** Generally made of steel, these round-bottomed pans allow the heat to spread rapidly and evenly, which is essential in Chinese cooking. They are available with both wooden and steel handles—both styles should be used with a glove. Woks can be used for stir-frying, deep-frying, boiling and steaming.

**Bamboo steamer** Small steamer placed on wooden trivet; used with wok lid or its own bamboo lid.

**Chopsticks** The Chinese use long wooden chopsticks in cooking because they don't conduct heat.

**Seasoning the wok** Before using your wok for the first time, heat it over high heat, then brush it lightly with oil. Wipe clean with paper towels before repeating the procedure two more times. Rinse well and dry thoroughly. The wok will rust if not in constant use. If it does, scour the rust off, rinse and brush again with oil to return it to good condition.

**Bamboo strainer** Bamboo-handled strainers are the best for lifting ingredients from steam or hot oil.

**Wok stand** Used to provide a secure base for the wok when it's used for steaming or deep-frying. It can be dispensed with when stir-frying as frying with a wok stand takes longer. Note: Although wok cookery is more suited to gas, it is possible to use electricity successfully. However, the food in the wok will take longer to reach the desired temperature. Unless you use a wok with a small, flattened bottom it is usually necessary to use a wok stand on an electric stove, especially for steaming and deep-frying.

**Wok scoop** Used to toss and turn ingredients when stir-frying.

# Steamers and Cleavers

There are two basic types of steamer: specially designed metal ones that act as both water boilers and food containers, and traditional-style bamboo steamers which fit on top of a wok, in which the water is boiled. These come in various sizes, from small (see page 28) for *dim sum* to those large enough to hold a whole fish (see below). The other method of steaming doesn't require a steamer but is just as effective, especially for everyday use (see page 43). Instead, the food (on a heatproof plate) is held above the water in the wok by a metal or bamboo trivet, and the steam is retained by a tightly fitting wok lid. For any cutting, fine or rough, all you need is a medium-weight cleaver and a solid wooden board.

**Assembled metal steamer** Slotting snugly together so that all the steam is directed up through the holes to the food, this steamer can sit directly on the heat.

**Bamboo steamer in wok** This traditional-style steamer can be used with one or more baskets to hold the food. The wok must rest on a wok rim for stability.

**Steamer** Made of stainless steel or aluminum, this specially designed steamer has a lower container for the water, on which sit one or two perforated containers for the food. The food is placed on a heatproof dish or muslin, and then covered with a tightly fitting lid.

**Cleaver** One of medium weight, about 3½ by 8 inches (8.5 by 20 centimeters), made of carbon or stainless steel is ideal for general use. If you find this too big, try a slender, lighter cleaver (see below). In China, this type is frequently used to carve Peking duck.

**Bamboo mat** To prevent meat from sticking during slow cooking, it should be placed on this latticed mat, which is placed inside the cooking pot.

**Chinese chopping board** A solid, wooden base is essential for chopping, and one 2 inches (5 centimeters) thick and 11 to 12 inches (28 to 30 centimeters) in diameter is ideal. When new, it should be soaked in water and oiled frequently to prevent splitting.

# Cutting vegetables

In Chinese cooking, all vegetables are cut up into uniformly small pieces, because this allows them to cook quickly without losing their crunchiness; it also means that they can absorb the taste of the oil and seasonings, despite the short cooking time. Some vegetables are cut according to their natural shape (for example, broccoli and cauliflower are cut into florets); others are sliced, shredded, diced or roll cut depending on the dish. For stir-frying, Chinese celery cabbage is shredded, but for braising, it is cut into larger pieces. Bamboo shoots, if braised, are cut into wedges, but if put into a stir-fried dish they are sliced thin. Chinese mushrooms can be sliced thin or thick, quartered or cut into small cubes. Root vegetables such as carrots and white radishes are roll cut to expose as many surfaces to the heat as possible; celery is traditionally cut on the diagonal to make it look more attractive.

**HOLDING THE CLEAVER  Method 1** Curl your fingers tightly around the handle, which should rest in the palm of your hand. This way, the cleaver will cut downward with its own weight.

**Method 2** Hold the handle in your palm as before, but slide your index finger down the side of the blade. Your thumb and forefinger then give you more control.

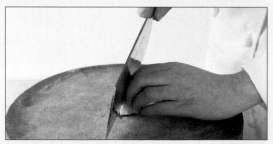

**GUARDING**  Hold the food with your fingertips turned under, knuckles forward so that they act as a guide for the cutting blade. Never lift the cleaver higher than your knuckles.

**SLICING**  Put the blade about ⅛ inch (3 millimeters) from one edge and slice downward. Regulate thickness by moving your fingers farther away from, or nearer to, the edge being cut.

**SHREDDING** Cut the food into uniform slices about ⅛ to ¼ inch (3 to 5 millimeters) wide, depending on preference. Cut across these slices to form shreds. With vegetables other than cabbage, stack the slices before slicing into strips.

**DIAGONAL CUTTING** Hold the top of the food firmly, with your fingers at a slant of 60°. Cut down at this angle and continue down to the end of the vegetable.

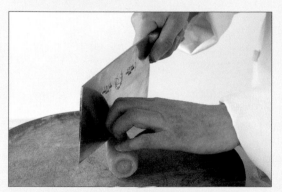

**ROLL CUTTING 1** Hold one end of the vegetable firmly and make a diagonal cut.

**2** Roll the vegetable a quarter turn toward you and make another diagonal cut. Continue rolling and cutting.

**RECONSTITUTING MUSHROOMS 1** Rinse the mushrooms. Put them in a bowl and pour on enough warm water to cover by about 1½ inches (3.5 centimeters).

**2** Set aside for about 20 to 30 minutes or until the mushrooms have become swollen and soft.

**CHOPPING CUCUMBER 1** Cut the cucumber diagonally into slices about ⅛ inch (3 millimeters) wide.

**2** Stack a few pieces together at a time and cut into sticks about ⅕ inch (5 millimeters) wide.

## CUTTING SCALLIONS

**BRUSHES 1** Trim the white ends of the scallions into 2½-inch (6-centimeter) lengths. Make repeated cuts through both ends, leaving the central section intact.

**2** Place the scallions in iced water and refrigerate for several hours. This will make the ends curl up, forming the brushes.

**SILKEN THREADS** Cut off the roots and any withered tops. Chop into 2- to 3-inch (5- to 7.5-centimeter) lengths. Slice along the length of the scallions and then cut the two halves into strands.

**FIVE-WAY SCALLIONS Top:** trimmed; **middle left:** sliced; **middle center:** silken threads; **middle right:** brushes; **bottom left:** small rounds; **bottom right:** diagonal cut.

# CUTTING GARLIC AND GINGER

**SILKEN THREADS  1** Slice thinly. Arrange the slices on top of each other.

**2** Placing the cleaver carefully, cut the slices into narrow strips.

**CRUSHING GARLIC  1** Lay the unpeeled cloves on a wooden board. Using the side of the cleaver, bang down on the garlic firmly.

**2** Separate the flesh from the skin by peeling one from the other.

**FINELY CHOPPED**  Place the garlic on a wooden board. Crush with the cleaver, remove the skin, then chop repeatedly until finely minced.

**THREE-WAY GARLIC AND GINGER  Top:** ginger root: sliced; silken threads; chopped fine. **Bottom:** garlic cloves: sliced; silken threads; chopped fine.

# Cutting meat

Because Chinese cooking methods rely on the rapid cooking of ingredients, any meat used has to be cut up into small, uniform pieces. Invariably for stir-frying, and sometimes for steaming, the meat should be cut up into thin slices, matchstick strips or cubes. This way it can be quickly stir-fried or steamed without losing any of its tenderness. Beef should always be cut across the grain or it will be tough; pork and chicken can be cut either along or across the grain. Although the cutting up of meat into small pieces is time-consuming, it is an integral part of Chinese cooking and is essential if you want the meat to taste good.

**MATCHSTICK CUT  1** Cut the meat into thin slices about ⅛ inch (3 millimeters) thick.

**2** Lay the slices on top of each other and cut them into narrow slivers like matchsticks.

**RECTANGULAR CUT  1** Cut the meat into manageable pieces about 1½ inches (3.5 centimeters) wide.

**2** Turn the chunks on their sides and then cut across the grain into rectangular slices about ¼ inch (5 millimeters) thick.

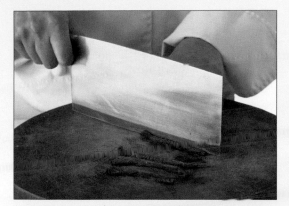

**SLIVERED CUT** Cut ⅕-inch (5-millimeter) slices of beef. Lay them flat and cut into long slivers. Use especially for Dry-fried beef.

**PAPER-THIN CUT** Slice the meat as thinly as possible. Freezing the meat for a couple of hours beforehand makes this easier.

**MATCHSTICK HEADS 1** Slice the ham into uniform strips. Gather the strips together so that they're lying parallel to one another.

**2** Hold the strips firmly with your free hand and cut across them to form small dice.

**CUBED CHICKEN 1** Cut the breast lengthwise into three long strips.

**2** Gather the strips together and cut across them to form uniform cubes.

**MARCH-CHOPPING 1** Cut the meat into small pieces. Using one or two cleavers, rhythmically chop the meat, moving from side to side.

**2** As the meat spreads, slip a cleaver under one side and use it to flip the meat into the center. Then continue chopping.

## SPECIAL TECHNIQUES

**DEVEINING PRAWNS 1** Shell the prawns. Hold the tail end firmly and make a small cut along the center of the back.

**2** Remove the black vein and discard it.

**MINCING PRAWNS 1** Shell and devein the prawns and cut up roughly. Using the broad side of the cleaver, press down on the prawns to flatten them.

**2** Repeatedly chop the prawns until they're minced.

# CHOPPING POULTRY CHINESE-STYLE

**1** Slice off the leg on each side, cutting down through the joint close to the body.

**2** On each leg cut the drumstick and thigh apart. Cut both the thigh and the drumstick in two.

**3** Split the carcass in half lengthwise so that the back and breast form two separate pieces.

**4** Remove the breastbone with a knife, sliding it between the bone and the meat.

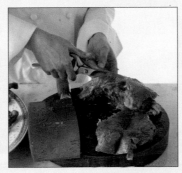

**5** Using a pair of kitchen scissors cut the backbone out of the back piece, and discard.

**6** Cut the back pieces crosswise into 1-inch (2.5-centimeter) pieces.

**7** Halve the breast meat lengthwise then cut crosswise into 1-inch (2.5-centimeter) pieces.

**8** Reassemble the bird with the breast meat on top of the back pieces.

# Shredded Chicken with Tientsin Fen Pi

## INGREDIENTS

2 cups clear stock or water
2 small chicken breasts, skinned
  and boned, or chicken breast fillet
4 pieces Tientsin fen pi, each about
  9 inches (23 centimeters) in diameter
½ long cucumber, about 8 ounces
  (225 grams)

### For the sauce

1 tablespoon rice or white wine vinegar
2 teaspoons hot prepared mustard
½ teaspoon salt
½ teaspoon sugar
4 tablespoons thin soy sauce
8 turns white pepper mill
1 tablespoon sesame oil
3 tablespoons peanut or corn oil

**SERVES 6**

This pleasant Northern dish is served cold with a slightly tangy sauce, and because it can be prepared completely in advance it is very handy for entertaining. The *fen pi*, literally meaning the skin of flour, must not be soggy if the dish is to be successful.

**1** Put the stock or water in a saucepan and bring to a boil. Add the chicken and simmer, covered, for about 5 minutes. Remove from the heat and let steep in the liquid for 15 minutes without disturbing. Remove and let cool.

**2 Prepare the sauce:** Mix together the vinegar, mustard, salt, sugar, soy sauce, pepper and oils.

**3** Bring a large pan of water, about 6 cups, to a fast boil. Put in the fen pi, one by one, so that they will not stick to each other. Cover and remove from the heat for 5 minutes. Drain. Then, handling with care, put the fen pi into a pan of cold water.

**4** Fold each fen pi into 3, then cut crosswise at ½-inch (1-centimeter) intervals. Transfer to a serving plate.

**5** Cut the cucumber diagonally into thin slices, leaving them in an ordered pile. Cut the pile into thin strips. Place on top of the fen pi.

**6** Going with the grain, tear the chicken by hand into thin strips and put on top of the cucumber.

**7** Just before serving, pour the sauce over it, mix well and serve.

**Note:** If the dish is not to be served right away, the ingredients can be individually refrigerated, covered, and assembled just prior to serving.

# Edible Jellyfish with Cucumber

## INGREDIENTS

1 pound (450 grams) preserved
  edible jellyfish
½ long cucumber

**For the dressing**
1 teaspoon rice or cider vinegar
2 tablespoons thin soy sauce
½ teaspoon sugar
1 tablespoon sesame oil
½ teaspoon prepared mustard

**SERVES 4**

Do not be put off by the initial rubbery appearance of the jellyfish, which is sold in sheets, folded and packed into plastic bags with large grains of salt in between the folds. When properly prepared, edible jellyfish gives great pleasure to those who enjoy food as much for texture as for taste. This is certainly why the Chinese like it.

**1** Shake all the sandy salt from the jellyfish. Wash in 3 changes of water, squeezing to get rid of some of the excess saltiness.

**2** Put into a large, deep bowl and fill with cold water. Soak for 3 to 4 days, changing the water twice a day and squeezing the jellyfish each time. At the end of the soaking, it should be totally free of salt.

**3 Prepare the dressing:** Mix together the vinegar, soy sauce, sugar, oil and mustard.

**4** Squeeze excess water from the jellyfish. Put on a board and cut into thin strips about ⅛ inch (3 millimeters) wide. Drain well.

**5** Cut the cucumber diagonally into slices about ⅛ inch (3 millimeters) thick. Stack a few pieces together at a time and cut into sticks about ⅕ inch (5 millimeters) wide.

**6** Arrange the cucumber sticks in a circle on the serving plate and place the jellyfish in the center.

**7** Just before serving, add the well-stirred dressing to the jellyfish.

# Steamed Scallops in the Shell

## INGREDIENTS

20 large scallops
peanut or corn oil for deep-frying
6 or 8 cloves garlic, peeled and diced
4 or 6 large scallions, green parts only,
  cut into rounds

### For the sauce

4 or 6 large scallions, white parts only,
  cut into silken threads (see page 34)
3 to 4 tablespoons peanut or corn oil
¾ inch (2 centimeters) fresh ginger root,
  peeled and cut into silken threads
  (see page 35)
3 or 4 fresh green chilies, seeded and
  cut into rounds
2 tablespoons thick soy sauce
2 tablespoons thin soy sauce
2 tablespoons water

**SERVES 6 TO 8**

A Cantonese dish at its simplest and best. The fresh scallops are steamed with just a touch of garlic, then served with a sauce to add zest to their natural sweetness. The details of preparation, seemingly elaborate, are nevertheless worth observing if you wish to make this simple yet sophisticated dish.

**1** Ask the fishdealer to open the scallops on the cup side of the shells rather than on the flat side. If they have already been opened on the flat side, ask for the cup shells, so that you can transfer the scallop meat to them. Remove the frills or rims, sandy and black impurities and the muscles, leaving only the white meat and the corals or roes. Separate the corals from the meat and save them for another recipe or freeze them. Rinse the scallop meat and pat dry, leaving them on the shells.

**2 Prepare the sauce:** Divide the scallions into 2 portions and put into 2 serving bowls. Heat a wok until smoke rises. Add the oil and swirl it around. Lower the heat and add the ginger and chilies. Remove from the heat. After a few seconds, add the soy sauces and water and bring to simmering point. Pour this mixture over the scallions in the bowls.

**3** Half fill a wok or deep fryer with oil. Heat to a temperature of 350°F (180°C) or until a cube of stale bread browns in 60 seconds. Put the garlic into a small wire sieve. Dip the sieve into the oil quickly 3 or 4 times, or until the garlic has taken on color. Save the oil for the other deep-frying purposes.

**4** Place 4 or 5 pieces of garlic and the same amount of green scallions on each scallop. Place the scallops in a wok or steamer; some shells can perch on top of other shells as long as they are not pressing down on the meat.

**5** Steam over high heat for about 7 to 10 minutes. The scallops will be opaque and be just cooked. There will be juice in the shell.

**6** Remove each shell, taking care not to spill the juice, and put on a large serving platter or on individual plates. Serve hot.

**7** To eat, put a small amount of sauce on the meat, then break it up to absorb the sauce. As host or hostess, do encourage your guests to pick up the shell and drink the tasty juice as well.

# Deep-fried Phoenix-tail Prawns

## INGREDIENTS

1 pound (450 grams) fresh or frozen
  medium raw prawns in the shell,
  without heads
½ teaspoon salt
few turns white pepper mill
1 large green pepper, seeded
peanut or corn oil for deep-frying

**For the batter**

5 ounces (140 grams) all-purpose flour
5 tablespoons cornstarch
1½ teaspoons baking powder
1 cup water
½ teaspoon salt
2 tablespoons peanut or corn oil

SERVES 6

This dish derives its name from the Chinese emblem of beauty, the phoenix. Prawns are likened to its long and graceful tail.

**1  Prepare the batter:** Sift the flour and cornstarch into a large bowl, add the baking powder. Gradually whisk in the water and blend to a smooth consistency. Let stand for a minimum of 30 minutes. Just before using, add the salt and blend in the oil until the batter is smooth and shiny.

**2**  If frozen prawns are used, defrost thoroughly. Remove the shells but leave the tail intact. Devein (see page 38) and pat dry with paper towels.

**3**  Turn the prawns upside down, one by one, and make 3 slashes across the abdomen without cutting through completely. This prevents them from curling up when deep-fried. Add the salt and pepper.

**4**  Cut the green pepper into rectangular pieces.

**5**  Half fill a wok or deep fryer with oil. Heat to a temperature of 375°F (190°C), or until a cube of stale bread browns in 50 seconds.

**6**  Hold the prawn by its tail and coat the rest of its body in the batter. Lift by the tail and let some of the runny batter drip off. Put into the oil. Add about half of the prawns at a time or as many as will float freely. Deep-fry for about 3 minutes, or until the batter is pale golden in color. Remove with a hand strainer or perforated spoon and drain on paper towels. Snip off any "bearded" excess batter with a pair of scissors.

**7**  While the prawns are in the oil, put half of the green pepper in the batter and add to the oil to fry with the prawns. Remove them when they look pale golden in color and drain on paper towels.

**8**  Deep-fry the remaining prawns and green pepper.

**9**  To serve, pile the green pepper in the middle of a platter and arrange the prawns around it with their tails facing outward.

**Note:** To reheat, either deep-fry the prawns and green pepper for about 30 seconds, until the batter is crisp again, or put under a preheated grill.

# Stuffed Crab Claws

## INGREDIENTS

1¼ pounds (560 grams) fresh or frozen
   medium raw prawns in the shell,
   without heads
3 ounces (85 grams) of fatback
4 tablespoons cornstarch
12 medium fresh or frozen cooked
   and shelled crab claws
peanut or corn oil for deep-frying

**For the marinade**
1 teaspoon salt
½ teaspoon sugar
1 teaspoon cornstarch
1 egg white, lightly beaten
1 teaspoon sesame oil

**For the dips**
chili sauce
Worcestershire sauce

**SERVES 6**

Biting into crabmeat and prawn at the same time produces a rich and luxurious feeling. These crisp and juicy crab claws are as good to look at as they are to eat, so they are bound to be a successful starter for a dinner party. You can prepare in advance up to the end of step 6, and then simply recrisp the claws just before serving.

**1** If frozen prawns and crab claws are used, defrost thoroughly. Shell and devein the prawns (see page 38). Pat dry with paper towels.

**2** Chop the prawns and fatback by hand or mince coarsely. Put in a bowl.

**3 Prepare the marinade:** Add the salt, sugar and cornstarch to the prawns and fatback. Stir vigorously for about 1 minute, or until the mixture becomes sticky. Add the egg white and stir again for about 1 minute, or until the paste is firm and elastic. Cover and let marinate in the refrigerator for about 30 minutes. Blend in the sesame oil.

**4** Put the 4 tablespoons of cornstarch in a bowl. Holding the pincers of one crab claw, dip the meaty part in the cornstarch: shake off any excess. Repeat with the rest of the claws.

**5 Stuff the claws:** Divide the paste into 12 portions. Lightly oil a plate. Holding the claw by the pincers, press a portion of the paste on the meat, covering a small area of the shell to seal it. Place on the lightly oiled plate. Repeat with the rest of the claws. To prevent your fingers from getting too sticky, wet them with cold water.

**6** Half fill a wok or deep fryer with oil. Heat to a temperature of 350°F (180°C), or until a cube of stale bread browns in 60 seconds. Carefully lower 6 claws into the oil, 1 at a time. Deep-fry for about 4 minutes, or until golden, turning each one occasionally. Remove each claw with a perforated spoon or tongs and drain on paper towels. Repeat with the remaining 6 claws.

**7** Deep-fry all 12 claws together for a few seconds to crisp. Remove and drain. Serve the claws immediately. Pass the dips in separate saucers.

# Ginger Soup with Pork and Wood Ears

### INGREDIENTS

½ ounce (15 grams) wood ears, reconstituted (see page 33)
6 ounces (175 grams) lean pork
2 to 3 tablespoons peanut or corn oil
1 to 2 ounces (25 to 55 grams) fresh ginger root, peeled and sliced into slivers
1 tablespoon Shaohsing wine or medium-dry sherry
½ teaspoon salt
2 teaspoons thin soy sauce
4 cups clear stock
3 scallions, cut into ½-inch (1-centimeter) pieces

**SERVES 6**

This is a favorite summer soup of the Hunanese, who appreciate the cooling effect that the ginger brings on a humid day.

**1** Drain excess water from the wood ears but leave damp. Break up the larger pieces.

**2** Slice the pork into strips, about 1½ by ½ inch (3.5 by 1 centimeters) and ¹⁄₁₀ inch (2 millimeters) thick.

**3** Heat a wok over high heat until smoke rises. Add the oil and swirl it around. Add the ginger and stir a few times. Put in the pork and, sliding the wok scoop or metal spatula to the bottom of the wok, turn and toss for about 30 seconds. Add the wood ears, lowering the heat so they do not make explosive sounds or fly out of the wok. Stir and turn for another 30 seconds.

**4** Add the wine or sherry, salt, soy sauce and stock. Bring to a boil. Spoon off the foam that surfaces. Lower the heat, cover and simmer for 10 to 15 minutes. Taste for seasoning, then add the scallions and immediately remove from the heat.

**5** Transfer to a large warm soup tureen or individual soup bowls and serve hot.

# Wonton Wrapper Crisps Soup

### INGREDIENTS

peanut or corn oil for deep-frying

60 wonton wrappers, halved and folded in 2

8 ounces (225 grams) Cantonese roast duck with some skin, diced (see pages 198–9)

10 ounces (280 grams) cooked crabmeat, broken into chunks

4 ounces (115 grams) canned bamboo shoots, sliced or diced thin

8 ounces (225 grams) canned straw mushroom, drained and halved or quartered

9 cups prime or clear stock (see page 242)

1 to 2 teaspoons salt

pepper to taste

1 to 2 tablespoons thin soy sauce

12 scallions, cut diagonally into ½-inch (1-centimeter) pieces, white and green parts separated

**SERVES 10 TO 12**

The tender wonton wrappers, deep-fried to a crisp before being dunked in the soup, lend special character to this dish. The color of the ingredients, suspended in the clear soup, is especially attractive.

**1** Half fill a wok or a deep fryer with oil. Heat to a temperature of about 350°F (180°C), or until a cube of stale bread browns in 60 seconds. Add a batch of wonton wrappers, about 20 at a time; they will sizzle and expand at once. Transfer to paper towels before they turn brown, using a hand strainer or perforated spoon. Repeat until all are done.

**2** Put the duck, crabmeat, bamboo shoots and straw mushrooms into the stock and bring to a boil. Add the salt, pepper and soy sauce. Add the white scallions and, finally, the wonton wrappers. (It is always better to add the wonton wrappers at the last moment so that they retain their crispness.) Dunk them with a wooden spoon. Remove from the heat and add the green scallions.

**3** Serve immediately, either from a communal bowl or in individual bowls.

**Note:** Wonton wrappers can be deep-fried ahead of time and, if kept in an airtight container, will remain crisp for more than a week. With some salt sprinkled on them, they are quite a novelty to serve with drinks. Cantonese roast duck (pages 198–9) is available in some Cantonese restaurants, whole or in portions.

# Cantonese Fire Pot

## INGREDIENTS

12 ounces to 1 pound (350 to 450
   grams) fresh or frozen medium raw
   prawns in the shell, without heads
1 Dover sole, or sea bass, about 1 pound
   (450 grams), skinned and boned
10 large scallops, white meat only
2 chicken breasts, skinned and boned
12 ounces to 1 pound (350 to 450
   grams) beef, rump, skirt steak or fillet
1 pound (450 grams) Chinese celery
   cabbage
1 large romaine lettuce
1 pound (450 grams) spinach, washed and
   trimmed
1 bunch watercress, washed and trimmed
4 cakes bean curd
1 pound (450 grams) dried egg noodles or
   1½ pounds (675 grams) fresh noodles
about 8 to 9 cups clear stock
peanut or corn oil

**For the dips**
8 eggs
thick or thin soy sauce
peanut, corn or sesame oil
salt
freshly ground black pepper
hot prepared mustard
chili sauce

**SERVES 8** as dinner

A Cantonese fire pot reflects what's easily available in the region, and it therefore consists of seafood as well as meat and vegetables. If you don't have a traditional charcoal-burning fire pot for cooking at the table, use a fondue set or heatproof bowl and burner or an electric pot.

**1** Shell and devein the prawns (see page 38). Halve lengthwise.

**2** Cut the fish fillets across into 1-inch (2.5-centimeter) pieces.

**3** Wash and pat dry the scallops. Remove and discard the hard muscles. Place each one on its side and cut into 3 or 4 pieces.

**4** Cut the chicken into thin slices, about ⅛ inch (3 millimeters) thick.

**5** Cut the beef across the grain into slices about 2 by 1½ inches and ¼ inch (5 by 3.5 centimeters and 5 millimeters) thick.

**6** Cut each Chinese celery cabbage stalk across at about 1-inch (2.5-centimeter) intervals.

**7** Break up the lettuce leaves into large pieces.

**8** Steep the bean curd in hot water for 15 minutes. Drain and cut each into 8 pieces.

**9** Bring a large pan of water to a boil. Add the noodles, return to a boil and continue to cook for a few minutes, or until *al dente*. Pour into a colander and refresh under cold running water. Drain thoroughly.

**10** Arrange all the ingredients on individual plates or together on several plates. The meat and seafood slices can be laid overlapping each other. Put on the table.

**11** Arrange dips in small dishes. Put on the table, with the fire pot in the center.

**12** To serve, provide each person with one bowl and a side plate, one pair of bamboo chopsticks and one small wire strainer.

**13** Crack 1 egg into each bowl and beat lightly. Pour 2 teaspoons of soy sauce on each saucer and add ½ teaspoon of oil. This can be replenished by individuals later.

**14** Have the stock simmering in a saucepan.

**15** If a traditional fire pot is used, heat the charcoal and put into the chimney in the middle of the pot. Put on the table on top of a thick heatproof mat. An electric pot may be used. In either case, pour sufficient stock into the heated pot to come about halfway up the sides, and bring back to a boil. Add about 3 tablespoons of oil.

# Steamed Prawns in Mixed Bean Sauce

## INGREDIENTS

12 ounces (350 grams) medium or large
   prawns in the shell, without heads
a few coriander leaves, torn into pieces

**For the sauce**
1 tablespoon fermented black beans
1 tablespoon salted yellow beans
½ teaspoon sugar
1 teaspoon sesame oil
4 to 5 tablespoons peanut or corn oil
4 to 6 cloves garlic, peeled
   and chopped fine
½ to ¾ inch (1 to 2 centimeters) fresh
   ginger root, peeled and chopped fine
½ to 1 fresh green or red chili, seeded
   and sliced into tiny rounds
1 to 1½ tablespoons Shaohsing wine or
   medium-dry sherry

**SERVES 4 TO 6** with 2 or 3 other dishes

I first tasted this dish in 1980 in one of the famous restaurants of my
hometown, Hong Kong, and thought it tasted heavenly. There was no
question of their letting me into their cookery secret, so I experimented
and came up with this concoction. I think you will enjoy it, too.

**1 Prepare the sauce:** Mash the black beans and salted yellow beans
together with the sugar and sesame oil into a paste.

**2** Heat a wok over high heat until smoke rises. Add the oil and swirl it around.
Add the garlic, and as soon as it takes on color, put in the ginger. Stir. Quickly
add the mashed bean paste, stir well, and then add the chili. Splash in the wine
or sherry around the side of the wok. As soon as the sizzling dies down, lower
the heat, stir well and then pour the sauce into a container and allow to cool.

**3** Remove and discard the prawn legs. Pat dry. Split lengthwise into 2, except
for the tails. Discard the veins. Arrange around a heatproof serving dish with a
slightly raised edge.

**4** Spoon the sauce on the prawns, scraping up every bit of oil as well.

**5** Steam in a wok or steamer, over moderately high heat for 3 or 4 minutes
(see page 43). Check to see if the prawns are cooked. Scatter the coriander
leaves over the prawns. Replace the lid and steam for a brief moment, to
cook the coriander leaves partially.

**6** Remove from the heat and again spoon the sauce on the prawns
and coriander leaves. Serve immediately from the dish in which they
were cooked.

# Abalone with Chinese Mushrooms

## INGREDIENTS

16 dried Chinese mushrooms (the thick and floral ones are best), washed
1 medium iceberg lettuce, washed and trimmed
1 can best abalone, 15 to 16 ounces (425 to 450 grams)
drained can juice from abalone
5 tablespoons peanut or corn oil
3 scallions, cut into 1-inch (2.5-centimeter) sections, white and green parts separated
1 tablespoon Shaohsing wine or medium-dry sherry
3 tablespoons oyster sauce
1½ teaspoons thick soy sauce
½ teaspoon sugar
1 tablespoon potato flour, dissolved in 2 tablespoons water

**SERVES 4** with 2 other dishes

Dried abalone, which ranks with shark's fin and bird's nest in gastronomic prestige, is sadly out of the question for most people's pockets; these days canned abalone graces even the best tables. Although it lacks the depth of taste found in dried abalone, its subtle taste and slightly chewy texture satisfy the palate of many a gourmet.

**1** Put the mushrooms in a saucepan and pour over them 3 cups of boiling water. Return to a boil, then lower the heat and simmer for 1 hour, until tender. When cool, clip off the stems and discard. Squeeze out excess water but leave damp. (They can be prepared hours ahead of time.)

**2** Tear the lettuce leaves into large pieces.

**3** Drain the abalone, reserving the juice. Slice it into pieces about ⅛ inch (3 millimeters) thick.

**4** Pour the can juice into a saucepan, add 1 tablespoon of the oil and bring to a boil. Immerse the lettuce in it, return to a boil and cook for 1 minute; the lettuce will be cooked yet still crisp. Transfer with a perforated spoon to a sieve placed over a bowl, so that it will continue to drain. Pour the drained stock back into the saucepan.

**5** Heat a wok over high heat until smoke rises. Add the remaining oil and swirl it around. Add the white scallions and stir a couple of times. Splash in the Shaohsing wine or sherry around the side of the wok, then add the stock saved from the lettuce, the oyster sauce, thick soy sauce, to enhance the coloring, and sugar. Bring to a boil.

**6** Add the mushrooms and abalone and slowly return to a boil. Cover, lower the heat and simmer for about 2 minutes, to let the abalone and mushrooms absorb the flavor.

**7** Spread the lettuce on a warm serving plate.

**8** Trickle the well-stirred dissolved potato flour into the sauce, stirring as it thickens. Tip in the green scallions.

**9** Transfer the ingredients to the serving plate, arranging the mushrooms on the lettuce, cap side up, then the abalone. Pour the sauce over them. Serve hot.

# Deep-fried Fish with Sweet and Sour Sauce

## INGREDIENTS

1 red snapper or gray mullet, about 2¼ to
  2½ pounds (1 to 1.15 kilograms), cleaned
  with head left on
peanut or corn oil for deep-frying
1 egg yolk
about 3 tablespoons cornstarch

**For the marinade**

1 inch (2.5 centimeters) fresh ginger
  root, peeled and chopped fine
1 teaspoon Shaohsing wine or
  medium-dry sherry
1 teaspoon salt

**For the sweet and sour sauce**

3 dried Chinese mushrooms, reconstituted
  (see page 33)
2 ounces (55 grams) small peas
2 teaspoons potato flour, dissolved in
  2 tablespoons water
4 tablespoons rice or wine vinegar
4 tablespoons sugar
4 tablespoons tomato ketchup
1 teaspoon salt
1½ teaspoons thick soy sauce
2 teaspoons Shaohsing wine or
  medium-dry sherry
1 cup water
4 tablespoons peanut or corn oil
1 clove garlic, peeled and chopped fine
1 small onion or 3 shallots, skinned
  and diced
2 ounces (55 grams) canned bamboo
  shoots, diced

**SERVES 6** with 3 other dishes

A sweet and sour sauce goes especially well with deep-fried food, not just because it whets one's appetite but, more important, because it counteracts any trace of grease. Such is, indeed, the case with fish. There are regional variations and personal preferences, but mainly a sweet and sour sauce is a mixture of vinegar and sugar, balanced by salt, and made more interesting by the addition of other condiments. Try this one, and then concoct your own.

**1** If the wok in which the fish will be deep-fried is large enough (14 inches [35 centimeters] or more) leave the fish whole; otherwise, cut it in half. Make 2 or 3 diagonal slashes across the thickest part of both sides of the fish, taking care not to go right to the edges.

**2 Prepare the marinade:** Squeeze the ginger in a garlic press with 2 drops of water and mix the juice with the wine or sherry and salt. Rub both sides of the fish, including the crevices and the cavity, with the mixture. Let marinate for about 15 to 30 minutes. Discard any excess liquid.

**3 Prepare the sweet and sour sauce:** Drain and squeeze out excess water from the mushrooms but leave damp. Cut into small cubes. Cook the peas in boiling water for 2 minutes, drain. Mix together the dissolved potato flour, vinegar, sugar, ketchup, salt, soy sauce, wine or sherry and water. Heat a wok (if you have a second small one), or a saucepan, over high heat until smoke rises. Add 3 tablespoons of the oil and swirl it around. Add the garlic, then the onion or shallots and fry for about 1 minute, stirring. Add the mushrooms, peas and bamboo shoots. Stir the sauce mixture once more to blend, then pour into the wok or saucepan. Bring to a boil, stirring continuously as it thickens. Set aside.

**4** Half fill a wok or deep fryer with oil. Heat to a temperature of 375°F (190°C), or until a cube of stale bread browns in 50 seconds.

**5** While the oil is heating, brush the egg yolk over both sides of the fish, then sift the cornstarch over it, smoothing it for evenness.

**6** Lower the fish into the oil and deep-fry for about 7 or 8 minutes, or until the skin is crisp. Turn over carefully and deep-fry the other side for about the same time.

# Stir-fried Chinese Celery Cabbage with Dried Shrimp

## INGREDIENTS

1 ounce (25 grams) dried shrimp, rinsed

1 Chinese celery cabbage, about 2 pounds (900 grams)

3 or 4 tablespoons peanut or corn oil

4 scallions, cut into 1-inch (2.5-centimeter) sections, white and green parts separated

4 thin slices fresh ginger root, peeled

¼ to ½ teaspoon salt

**SERVES 4 TO 6** with 2 or 3 other dishes

This economical and healthy everyday dish is easy to make. It is as popular in Canton as in Shanghai, but the Cantonese use scallions, ginger and shrimp to heighten the flavor; in Shanghai they prefer just dried shrimp.

**1** Soak the shrimp in just enough boiling water to cover them, for 30 minutes or longer. Drain reserving the soaking liquid.

**2** Discard any wilted or hard outer leaves of the cabbage. Then put together similar-sized leaves. Chop crosswise into thin strips. Remove and discard the hard core.

**3** Heat a wok over high heat until smoke rises. Add the oil and swirl it around. Add the white scallions, stir a couple of times, then add the ginger. As they sizzle, add the shrimp, which will "explode" when they touch the oil, releasing a mouth-watering fragrance. Stir the shrimp for a few seconds.

**4** Add the cabbage and, sliding the wok scoop or metal spatula to the bottom of the wok, turn and toss for about 1 minute so that the cabbage will absorb the fragrance of the other ingredients. Adjust the heat if the cabbage begins to burn. Pour in the shrimp water, season with the salt, cover and continue cooking for 1 or 2 minutes, or until the cabbage is tender yet still crunchy. Add the green scallions. Transfer to a warm serving plate and serve immediately.

# Lobster with Ginger and Scallions

## INGREDIENTS

2 lobsters, each about 1½ pounds
   (675 grams)
peanut or corn oil for deep-frying
3 tablespoons peanut or corn oil
3 ounces (85 grams) fresh ginger root,
   peeled and cut into thin slices
10 to 12 large scallions, cut diagonally,
   white and green parts separated
1½ tablespoons Shaohsing wine or brandy
½ cup prime stock (see page 242)

**For the sauce**
1 teaspoon potato flour
4 tablespoons water
½ tablespoon thin soy sauce
1½ tablespoons oyster sauce

**SERVES 6** as a first course

The species of lobster found along the Chinese coast is the spiny lobster or crayfish and, significantly, the Chinese name for it is dragon prawn. The meat, compared to that of the true lobster, is slightly coarser, but cooking methods and recipes are the same for both. Only fresh lobsters are fit for consumption; they can be kept alive up to 3 days in the vegetable compartment of the refrigerator.

**1  Prepare the sauce:** Mix together the flour, water, soy sauce and oyster sauce. Set aside.

**2**  Kill and chop up the lobsters. Before starting, make sure that strong rubber bands are around the pincers. Lay the lobsters flat, one at a time, on a chopping board, and steady them with one hand. Pierce the center of the head, where there is a cross, with the pointed end of a strong knife, pressing firmly all the way down in order to paralyze the nerve and hence kill the lobster instantly. Split it in half along the back, all the way to the tail, cutting through both the shell and the flesh. Remove and discard the pouch of grit from the head, as well as the dark gut running along the body. Remove the tiny eggs, if any, and the greenish creamy substance (tomalley), which can be cooked separately if you like it. Twist the joints to dislodge the 2 claws from the body. Lay each half of the body flat and, using a kitchen cleaver, chop each into 3 pieces. Remove the gill from the head, close to the shell. Lay the claws on the board and bang them, one by one, with either the broad side of the cleaver or a hammer until the shell is cracked at various points so that it will not be necessary to use crackers when eating them. Cut each claw in two at its obvious joint.

**3**  Put all the head and claw pieces into one large bowl and the body pieces into another. Pat dry with paper towels.

**4**  Half fill a wok or deep fryer with oil. Heat to a temperature of 350°F (180°C), or until a cube of stale bread browns in 60 seconds. Carefully lower all the head and claw pieces into the oil and let them "go through the oil" for 20 to 30 seconds, so that their juices are sealed in. Remove immediately with a large hand strainer and put on a large platter.

**5**  Reheat the oil and let the body pieces "go through the oil" for about 10 seconds.

**6**  Empty the oil into a container and save it for other purposes. Wash and dry the wok.

# Kung Pao Chicken

A famous Szechwan dish that tempts the palate with a full range of tastes and aftertastes: peppery hot and spicy, savory and slightly sweet and sour. It is said that this was a favorite dish of a Szechwan governor during the Ch'ing dynasty (1644–1911), after whose official title, "Kung Pao," the dish was named. The governor must have been fond of peanuts, for it is unthinkable not to add them.

**1** Cut the chicken into thin strips. Cut into cubes about ½ inch (1 centimeter) square. Put into a bowl.

**2 Prepare the marinade:** Add the salt, soy sauce, wine or sherry, cornstarch and egg white to the chicken. Mix well and let marinate for 15 to 30 minutes.

**3 Prepare the sauce:** Mix together the soy sauce, chili sauce, vinegar, sugar, cornstarch, and stock or water.

**4** Heat a wok over high heat until smoke rises. Add the oil and swirl it around. Add the dried chili, stir, then add the garlic and ginger and stir to release their aroma. Add the chicken. Sliding the wok scoop or metal spatula to the bottom of the wok, turn and toss for about 60 seconds. Splash in the wine or sherry around the side of the wok, stirring and tossing continuously. Add the scallions and continue to stir for another 30 to 45 seconds. The chicken should be almost cooked by now.

**5** Add the well-stirred sauce to the wok. Continue to stir while it thickens.

**6** Add the peanuts, stir to mix for a few times, then transfer to a warm serving plate. Serve immediately.

## INGREDIENTS

12 ounces (350 grams) chicken breast meat
4 tablespoons peanut or corn oil
2 or 3 long (about 3 inches [7.5 centimeters] or more each) dried red chilies, or 4 or 5 smaller, seeded and cut into pieces
2 cloves garlic, peeled and diagonally sliced
4 to 6 thin slices fresh ginger root
1 tablespoon Shaohsing wine or medium-dry sherry
3 scallions, cut into small rounds
2 ounces (55 grams) roasted peanuts

### For the marinade
⅓ teaspoon salt
2 teaspoons thin soy sauce
2 teaspoons Shaohsing wine or medium-dry sherry
1 teaspoon cornstarch
1 tablespoon egg white, lightly beaten

### For the sauce
1 tablespoon thick soy sauce
1 or 2 tablespoons chili sauce
2 teaspoons rice or white wine vinegar
2 teaspoons sugar
1½ teaspoons cornstarch
6 tablespoons clear stock or water

**SERVES 4** with 3 other dishes

# Paper-wrapped Chicken

The wind-dried sausage in this dish makes the chicken, already highly seasoned in the marinade, even spicier and richer in taste.

## INGREDIENTS

the rest of the chicken (or 6 drumsticks or
   thigh pieces), over 2 pounds (900 grams)
12 small or 6 large dried Chinese
   mushrooms, recon page 33)
4 to 6 ounces (115 to175 grams) canned
   bamboo shoots
6 wind-dried Chinese sausages, liver
   or pork or both
24 pieces greaseproof paper, each
   8 inches (20 centimeters) square
24 large pieces coriander leaves (optional)
peanut or corn oil for deep-frying

**For the marinade**

3 tablespoons thin soy sauce
2 teaspoons sugar
2 teaspoons Shaohsing wine or
   medium-dry sherry
1 teaspoon ginger powder
¼ teaspoon five-spice powder
1 tablespoon sesame oil

**SERVES 8** as a first course;
**4** as a main course with a salad

**1** Skin and bone the drumsticks and thighs. Discard the pinions of the wings and chop each wing into 3 pieces. Scrape out the 2 oysters. Put into a bowl.

**2 Prepare the marinade:** Add the soy sauce, sugar, wine or sherry, ginger, five-spice powder and oil to the chicken. Mix well. Let marinate for a minimum of 1 hour, turning the pieces occasionally.

**3** Squeeze out excess water from the mushrooms but leave damp. Halve if small ones are used, quarter if large ones are used.

**4** Slice the bamboo shoots into 24 pieces, each ⅕ inch (5 millimeters) thick.

**5** Rinse the Chinese sausages and pat dry. Slice each diagonally into 8 pieces, making a total of 48.

**6** About 10 minutes before the wrapping, add the mushrooms and bamboo shoots to the chicken, so that they can absorb some of the marinade.

**7** Using a brush, thoroughly oil one side of 1 square of greaseproof paper. Put on a plate or work surface at an angle, like a diamond, and layer on it 1 piece of chicken between 2 slices of Chinese sausage, then 1 piece of bamboo shoot, and, finally, 1 piece of mushroom with a coriander leaf on top.

**8** To wrap in the classic Chinese way, fold the bottom flap up toward the center, then fold the 2 side flaps inward on top of each other and finally fold the top flap down and tuck it squarely inside the opening. Repeat this process until all have been wrapped.

**9** Half fill a wok or deep fryer with oil. Heat to a temperature of 350° to 375°F (180° to 190°C), or until a cube of stale bread browns in 50 to 60 seconds. Slip 12 parcels into the oil, unsealed side down, and deep-fry for about 5 minutes if you like the chicken just done, or for about 8 minutes if you like it much more cooked and slightly charred. Turn them over for the last minute of cooking.

**10** Remove with a large hand strainer and, holding it carefully above the oil, let excess oil from the parcels drain back into the wok or deep fryer. Put the parcels on a warm serving plate. Reheat the oil and deep-fry the remainder as before.

# Willow Chicken in Black Bean Sauce

## INGREDIENTS

about 1¾ pounds (790 grams), pieces
    chicken thigh, skinned and boned
2 small green peppers, seeded
1 to 2 fresh green chilies, seeded (optional)
6 tablespoons peanut or corn oil
5 or 6 cloves garlic, peeled and cut into
    silken threads (see page 35)
4 scallions, cut into 1-inch
    (2.5-centimeter) sections, white
    and green parts separated
3 tablespoons fermented black beans,
    rinsed and mashed
1 tablespoon Shaohsing wine or
    medium-dry sherry
little sesame oil (optional)
chili sauce (optional)

### For the marinade

½ teaspoon salt
½ teaspoon sugar
1 tablespoon thin soy sauce
8 turns black pepper mill
2 teaspoons Shaohsing wine or
    medium-dry sherry
1 teaspoon cornstarch
2 tablespoons egg white, lightly beaten
1½ tablespoons peanut or corn oil

### For the sauce

1 teaspoon cornstarch
4 tablespoons clear stock or water
2 teaspoons oyster sauce or
    1 teaspoon thick soy sauce

**SERVES 6** with 3 other dishes

This dish takes its name from the willowy strips of the chicken and pepper.

**1** Cut the chicken into strips, about ⅕ inch (5 millimeters) thick. Put into a bowl.

**2 Prepare the marinade:** Add the salt, sugar, soy sauce, pepper and wine or sherry to the chicken. Sprinkle with the cornstarch, add the egg white and stir to coat. Let marinate for 15 to 30 minutes. Blend in the oil.

**3** Slice the peppers into long and narrow strips.

**4** Slice the chilies into strips.

**5 Prepare the sauce:** Mix together the cornstarch, stock or water, oyster or soy sauce.

**6** Heat a wok until hot. Add 1 tablespoon of the oil and swirl it around. Add the pepper and stir and toss with the wok scoop or metal spatula constantly for about 2 minutes. When tender yet crunchy, transfer to a warm plate and keep warm.

**7** Wash and dry the wok.

**8** Heat the wok over high heat until smoke rises. Add the remaining oil and swirl it around. Add the garlic and when it sizzles and takes on color, add the chilies, white scallions and then the black bean paste. Stir to blend with the garlic. Put in the chicken and stir and toss the strips for 2 minutes, or until they turn whitish, scraping the paste from the bottom of the pan to coat.

**9** Splash in the wine or sherry around the side of the wok and let it sizzle, stirring continuously. When the sizzling dies down, lower the heat and add the well-stirred sauce to the chicken. Continue to stir as the sauce thickens. Add the pepper and green scallions and mix well. Remove to a warm plate and serve immediately. A little sesame oil can be sprinkled on top. For those who like an extra-hot flavor, chili sauce can be served at the table.

**Note:** In pursuit of gastronomic excellence, you can let the chicken "go through the oil" (see page 40) before stir-frying it in step 8. In that case, simply stir-fry for a shorter time.

# Smoked Duck, Szechwan Style

## INGREDIENTS

1 scant teaspoon saltpeter
1 oven-ready duck, about 5 pounds
   (2.25 kilograms)
1¾ tablespoons salt
6 ounces (175 grams) all-purpose flour
4 ounces (115 grams) brown sugar
4 tablespoons black tea leaves
2 pieces fresh ginger root, each
   ½ inch (1 centimeter), peeled and bruised
2 large scallions
1 whole star anise (8 segments)
1 ½ teaspoons Szechwan peppercorns
2 tablespoons Shaohsing wine or
   medium-dry sherry
peanut or corn oil for deep-frying
1 tablespoon sesame oil

**SERVES 6** with 3 other dishes

The various cooking processes used in this dish may seem too time-consuming, but the duck is at once made crispy and moist, smoky and aromatic.

**1**  Rub the salt thoroughly over the skin of the duck and inside the cavity, then rub the cavity only with saltpeter. Leave the duck in a cool place for about 10 hours or overnight.

**2**  Rinse the duck, especially the cavity, in plenty of hot water. Wipe dry. The duck is now ready for smoking.

**3**  Line a large wok with heavy-duty foil and place the flour, sugar and tea in the bottom. Place a metal trivet or bamboo stand on top. Place the duck on that, breast side up, and make sure that there is a gap between it and the smoking ingredients, to allow free circulation of smoke. Put the wok cover on tightly.

**4**  Turn the heat on high until you see smoke coming out, then adjust it, making sure that plenty of smoke continues to come out. Smoke for 15 minutes, turn the duck over and smoke, breast side down, for another 15 minutes. Remove from the heat.

**5**  When cool enough to handle, transfer to a large heatproof dish, breast side up. Put half of the ginger, scallions, star anise, peppercorns and wine or sherry into the cavity; put the other half on the breast.

**6**  Steam in a steamer or another wok for 1 to 1¼ hours (see page 43).

**7**  When cool enough to handle, transfer the duck to a rack and let cool. Remove and discard all the condiments. Dry with paper towels.

**8**  Half fill a wok or deep fryer with oil. Heat to a temperature of 375°F (190°C), or until a cube of stale bread browns in 50 seconds. Carefully lower the duck into the oil, breast side down, and deep-fry for 3 or 4 minutes, or until brown. With a wooden spoon or spatula in one hand and another inside the cavity, turn the duck over and deep-fry the other side until brown. Hot oil can also be spooned over the skin. Remove to a chopping board. Brush the sesame oil over the breast. The duck can be carved either in the Chinese way (see page 39) or by your usual method. Serve warm.

**Note:** If the duck is prepared in advance, it can be reheated in a preheated oven at 300°F (150°C) for 30 to 45 minutes, or until it's hot and the skin is crisp.

# Sautéed Chicken Livers

In this simple dish, with its slightly piquant taste, the livers are partially browned, so that they're crispy on the outside, but pink inside. As one of the dishes in a Chinese meal, rice would be served with it as usual, but as a main course, noodles or spaghetti would do equally well. A green salad could be served afterward.

**1** Slice each liver into 2 or 3 pieces. Place in a colander to wash and drain well. Put into a large bowl.

**2 Prepare the marinade:** Add the salt, sugar, soy sauce, pepper, Worcestershire sauce and wine or sherry to the livers. Stir to mix well and let marinate for 1 to 2 hours, stirring occasionally.

**3 Prepare the sauce:** Put the cornstarch in a small bowl, stir in 2 tablespoons of the stock or water and blend until smooth. Add the soy and Worcestershire sauces, and stir in the remaining stock or water.

**4** Just before ready to cook, sprinkle the livers with the cornstarch and stir to coat well.

**5** Heat a wok over high heat until smoke rises. Add the oil and swirl it around. Add the ginger and white scallions and let them sizzle. As soon as the scallions take on color, add the livers and brown for about 2 minutes, turning once or twice with a wok scoop or metal spatula to prevent sticking. Sprinkle with the wine or sherry, and when the sizzling has died down, lower the heat, cover and cook for about 2 minutes. Turn the livers over, add the green scallions, cover and continue to cook for about 2 more minutes.

**6** Pour the well-stirred sauce over the livers and stir until it thickens. Transfer to a warm serving plate. Serve immediately

**Note:** If pressed for time, instead of marinating the livers, pierce them with a fork to let the marinade permeate.

## INGREDIENTS

1½ pounds (675 grams) chicken livers, trimmed
1½ teaspoons cornstarch
6 or 7 tablespoons peanut or corn oil
2 to 2½ inches (5 to 6 centimeters) fresh ginger root, peeled and cut into slices
9 or 10 large scallions, sliced diagonally into ½ inch (1-centimeter) sections, white and green parts separated
1½ tablespoons Shaohsing wine or medium-dry sherry

### For the marinade

¾ teaspoon salt
¾ teaspoon brown sugar
1 tablespoon thick soy sauce
10 turns black pepper mill
2 teaspoons Worcestershire sauce
2 teaspoons Shaohsing wine or medium-dry sherry

### For the sauce

1½ teaspoons cornstarch
6 tablespoons clear stock or water
2 teaspoons thick soy sauce
1 teaspoon Worcestershire sauce

**SERVES 4** as a main course,
**8** with 3 or 4 other dishes

# Duck Stuffed with Myriad Condiments

## INGREDIENTS

12 to 15 scallions, white parts only, made
    into brushes (see page 34)
1 pound (450 grams) taro, peeled
1 oven-ready duck, 4 to 4½ pounds
    (1.8 to 2 kilograms)
1 tablespoon thick soy sauce

### For the sauce stuffing

¼ of whole dried tangerine peel, soaked
    in cold water, then cut into small pieces
4 cloves garlic, peeled and chopped fine
2 inches (5 centimeters) fresh ginger root,
    peeled and chopped fine
3 shallots, skinned and chopped fine
2 whole star anise (16 segments)
6 tablespoons crushed yellow bean sauce
5 tablespoons hoisin sauce
1 tablespoon sesame paste
1 teaspoon five-spice powder
2 teaspoons ginger powder
2 teaspoons salt
2 tablespoons sugar
1 tablespoon Mei-kuei-lu wine or gin

**SERVES 6** with 3 or 4 other dishes

The best time to serve this famous Cantonese dish is in the autumn and winter. The sauce resulting from this subtly balanced blend of seasonings is delicious.

**1 Prepare the sauce stuffing:** Mix together the tangerine peel, garlic, ginger, shallots, star anise, sauces, sesame paste, five-spice powder, ginger powder, salt, sugar and wine or gin. (This can be done hours in advance.)

**2** Make the scallion brushes and put them in a bowl of water and refrigerate. (This can also be done hours in advance.)

**3** Slice the taro into pieces about ½ inch (1 centimeter) thick. Lay them on a large heatproof dish with raised edges.

**4** The duck must be at room temperature, otherwise the steaming will take much longer. Dry both skin and cavity with paper towels. Chop off the pinions of the wings; save them for the stockpot.

**5** Spoon the sauce stuffing into the cavity. To seal the tail end, fold the parson's nose inward. If necessary, use a thin poultry skewer or bamboo stick to thread through the skin. To seal the neck end, fold the flap of neck skin over the neck cavity.

**6** Lay the duck on top of the taro on the heatproof dish, breast side up. Put the dish into a wok or steamer and steam (see page 43), tightly covered, for 1¼ to 1½ hours, or until the duck is tender yet still firm.

**7** Drain the scallion brushes and pat dry.

**8** Remove the dish from the steamer and transfer the duck to another dish. Brush the thick soy sauce over the skin to give it color.

**9** Turn the parson's nose outward or remove the skewer. Spoon the sauce stuffing into a saucepan.

**10** Transfer the taro to a warm serving platter and keep warm. Degrease the liquid remaining in the heatproof dish and pour it into the saucepan.

**11** Stir to blend the liquid and the sauce stuffing in the saucepan and simmer over low heat for 5 to 10 minutes. Strain through a sieve and discard the solids. Return this sauce to the saucepan and bring to a simmer again.

# Chicken in Yunnan Steam Pot

## INGREDIENTS

12 medium dried Chinese mushrooms,
  reconstituted (see page 33)
8 ounces (225 grams) best ham,
  trimmed of fat
1 oven-ready chicken, 3 to 3¼ pounds
  (1.3 to 1.5 kilograms)
1 to 1¼ teaspoons salt
4 to 6 turns white pepper mill
2 thickish slices fresh ginger root, peeled
2 scallions, quartered
1 tablespoon Shaohsing wine or
  medium-dry sherry
thin soy sauce (optional)

**SERVES 6** with 3 other dishes

A Yunnan steam pot is basically a pottery casserole dish about 8 inches
(20 centimeters) in diameter and 4 inches (10 centimeters) high with a cone-
shaped chimney in the center of the bowl. The pot, with its tightly fitting lid,
is placed in boiling water so that steam rises through the chimney to circulate
inside and cook the ingredients. Chicken cooked in this way is tender and
succulent, and the accompanying soup is pure and flavorful. The pot is
available in some Chinese shops, but, in a pinch, a double boiler can be used.

**1** Drain and squeeze out excess water from the mushrooms but leave damp.
Reserve the soaking liquid.

**2** Slice the ham into large pieces.

**3** Chop the chicken through the bones into serving pieces, using a kitchen
cleaver, a mallet and kitchen scissors, if necessary. Cut the wings, thighs and
drumsticks at the joints and slit the whole breast off from the back. Cut and
discard the pinions, then halve each wing at the joint. Halve each thigh and
drumstick crosswise. Halve the breast lengthwise, then cut each half crosswise
into 3 or 4 pieces. Do not use the back; save it for the stockpot.

**4** Bring a large saucepan of water to a boil and add the chicken pieces. Return
to a boil and continue to boil for about 2 minutes, so that the scum rises. Pour
into a colander and rinse the chicken to get rid of any remaining scum.

**5** Line the steam pot with the mushrooms, ham and chicken. Add the salt,
pepper, ginger, scallions and wine or sherry. Add sufficient water (including the
mushroom water) to come within 1 inch (2.5 centimeters) of the top of the
chimney of the pot. Put the lid on.

**6** Over moderate heat, place the steam pot on the rim of a small saucepan with
boiling water inside, leaving a gap between the water level and the bottom of
the steam pot. Cook for 1 to 1¼ hours without disturbing. Replenish the water
in the saucepan from time to time, removing the steam pot to do so if necessary.

**7** Remove from the heat. Spoon off excess fat, if any, on the surface.

**8** Take the steam pot to the dining table and serve from it. Use the soy sauce
as a dip if you like.

# Stir-fried Bean Sprouts with Shredded Pork

## INGREDIENTS

6 ounces (175 grams) lean pork
1 small green pepper, halved
   lengthwise and seeded
6 tablespoons peanut or corn oil
3 thin slices fresh ginger root, peeled and
   cut into silken threads (see page 35)
1 pound (450 grams) bean sprouts
½ teaspoon salt
2 or 3 cloves garlic, peeled and
   chopped fine
3 scallions, halved lengthwise, cut into
   2-inch (5-centimeter) sections, white
   and green parts separated
2 teaspoons Shaohsing wine or
   medium-dry sherry

**For the marinade**
¼ teaspoon salt
¼ teaspoon sugar
2 teaspoons thin soy sauce
4 turns white pepper mill
1 teaspoon Shaohsing wine or
   medium-dry sherry
½ teaspoon potato flour
1 tablespoon water

**For the sauce**
½ teaspoon potato flour
3 tablespoons water
2 tablespoons oyster sauce

**SERVES 4** with 2 other dishes

The combination of meat and vegetables is a regular occurrence in Chinese cooking. Even though a small amount of meat is used, it nevertheless adds so much taste and interest to the vegetables that it is worth the effort.

**1** Cut the pork into matchstick-sized pieces. Put into a bowl.

**2 Prepare the marinade:** Add the salt, sugar, soy sauce, pepper, wine or sherry, potato flour and water to the pork. Stir in the same direction to coat. Let marinate for about 20 minutes.

**3** Slice the green pepper lengthwise into thin strips.

**4 Prepare the sauce:** Mix together the potato flour, water and oyster sauce.

**5** Heat a wok over high heat until smoke rises. Add 3 tablespoons of the oil and swirl it around. Add the ginger, and as it sizzles, add the bean sprouts and green pepper. Season with the salt. Sliding the wok scoop or spatula to the bottom of the wok, turn and toss continuously over high heat for about 2½ to 3 minutes. The bean sprouts and green pepper will be cooked but still crunchy. Transfer to a warm serving plate and keep warm.

**6** Wash and dry the wok. Reheat over high heat until smoke rises. Add the remaining oil and swirl it around. Add the garlic, and as it sizzles and takes on color, add the white scallions. Stir a few times, then put in the pork. Turn and toss for about 30 seconds, or until the pork begins to turn opaque. Splash in the wine or sherry around the side of the wok. As it sizzles, continue to stir and turn for another 30 to 60 seconds, or until the pork is cooked. Lower the heat. Pour the well-stirred sauce on the pork, stirring as it thickens. Add the green scallions and stir a few more times. Scoop the pork mixture over the bean sprouts. Serve immediately.

# Sweet and Sour Pork

To many people, sweet and sour pork is synonymous with bad Chinese takeout food: lumps of chewy pork wrapped in thick batter, covered with a gluey and sickening sweet and sour sauce. However, when well made—crisp outside yet tender inside, topped with a well-balanced sweet and sour sauce—this is one of the most appetizing Cantonese dishes.

## INGREDIENTS

1 pound (450 grams) lean pork belly, skinned and trimmed of excess fat
½ teaspoon salt
1 teaspoon thin soy sauce
½ egg, lightly beaten
3 tablespoons cornstarch
peanut or corn oil for deep-frying
2½ tablespoons peanut or corn oil
1 clove garlic, peeled and minced
1 onion, skinned and roughly chopped
1 green pepper, halved, seeded and diced
4 ounces (115 grams) canned pineapple chunks, drained, juice reserved

**For the sauce**
2 teaspoons potato flour
4 tablespoons water
4 tablespoons pineapple juice
3 tablespoons rice or wine vinegar
4 to 4½ tablespoons sugar
¼ teaspoon salt
2 teaspoons thin soy sauce
2 tablespoons tomato ketchup
1½ teaspoons Worcestershire sauce

**SERVES 4 TO 6** with 2 or 3 other dishes

**1** Cut the pork into pieces about 1 by 1¼ by ¾ inches (2.5 by 3 by 2 centimeters). Put into a bowl.

**2** Add the salt and soy sauce and let marinate for 30 to 60 minutes. Stir in the egg to coat thoroughly.

**3** Dredge the pork, piece by piece, with the cornstarch, making sure it is evenly coated. It is not necessary to use up all the cornstarch.

**4** Half fill a wok or deep fryer with oil. Heat to a temperature of 350°F (180°C), or until a cube of stale bread browns in 60 seconds. Add the pork and deep-fry for about 1 minute in 1 or 2 batches; separate the pieces with a pair of chopsticks or a wooden spoon if they stick together. Drain on paper towels. This step can be done ahead of time.

**5 Prepare the sauce:** In a bowl, dissolve the potato flour in the water and pineapple juice. Add the vinegar, sugar, salt, soy sauce, ketchup and Worcestershire sauce and stir to blend. (This can be made in advance.)

**6** Heat a frying pan or saucepan (unless you have another wok) until hot. Add 1½ tablespoons of oil and swirl it around. Add the garlic and onion, stir a few times and then add the green pepper. Stir-fry for about 2 minutes over medium heat and season with salt, if desired. Add the pineapple chunks. Pour in the well-stirred sauce and bring to a boil slowly, stirring constantly.

**7** Reheat the oil for deep-frying to a higher temperature, 375°F (190°C), or until a cube of stale bread browns in 50 seconds. Add the pork and again deep-fry in one batch for about 2 or 3 minutes, to ensure that the outside is crisp and golden without the pork inside getting dry. Drain on paper towels and transfer to a warm serving plate. Reheat the sweet and sour sauce and stir in the remaining 1 tablespoon of oil. This prevents the sauce from being gluey. Pour the sweet and sour sauce over the pork. Serve immediately.

**Note:** When reheated, sweet and sour pork will be soggy but it will still taste good.

# Pearly Pork Balls

It is a misconception to think that every Hunan dish is spicy hot. On the contrary, many are not, and this dish, that derives its name from the glutinous rice that shines like little pearls on the pork balls, is one of them.

## INGREDIENTS

5 ounces (140 grams) white glutinous rice
4 medium dried Chinese mushrooms, reconstituted (see page 33)
2 tablespoons dried shrimp, rinsed
4 water chestnuts, fresh peeled or canned, drained
12 ounces (350 grams) pork, about 3 ounces (85 grams) fat and 9 ounces (250 grams) lean
½ teaspoon salt
8 turns white pepper mill
1 tablespoon potato flour
2 ounces (55 grams) lean ham

**SERVES 6** with 3 other dishes

**1** Rinse the rice, rubbing gently with your fingers in 3 or 4 changes of water, or until it is no longer milky. Drain.

**2** Soak in plenty of cold water for about 4 hours. Drain well and spread out in a shallow pan.

**3** Drain and squeeze out excess water from the mushrooms but leave damp. Chop into the size of matchstick heads.

**4** Soak the shrimp, in just enough boiling water to cover them, for 10 to 15 minutes. Drain them, reserving the soaking liquid.

**5** Chop fine or mince the shrimp and the water chestnuts.

**6** Chop the fat and lean pork by hand or mince coarsely.

**7** Combine the mushrooms, dried shrimp, water chestnuts and pork in a large bowl. Add the salt, pepper and potato flour. Stir in, a spoonful at a time, 3 tablespoons of water and the soaking liquid from the shrimp.

**8** Cut the ham into pieces the size of matchstick heads and mix with the rice in the pan.

**9** Pick up about 1 tablespoon of the pork mixture, roll it between your palms into a ball about the size of a Ping-Pong ball. Roll this ball over the rice and ham, making sure it is completely covered, and put it on a heatproof plate. Repeat until all the pork mixture is used. The pork balls will fill more than one plate.

**10** Steam the pork balls in a wok or steamer for 15 minutes (see page 43).

**11** Serve the pearly balls hot, either piled up neatly in a bowl or arranged on a warm serving plate.

# Beef with Preserved Tangerine Peel

### INGREDIENTS

5 or 6 pieces preserved tangerine peel
1 sweet orange
1½ pounds (675 grams) beef, rump, fillet
    or skirt steak, trimmed
4 tablespoons peanut or corn oil
1 inch (2.5 centimeters) fresh ginger
    root, peeled and cut into silken threads
    (see page 35)
6 scallions cut into 2-inch
    (5-centimeter) sections,
    white and green parts separated
1 tablespoon Shaohsing wine or
    medium-dry sherry
2 to 3 tablespoons chili sauce

**For the marinade**
¾ teaspoon salt
1 teaspoon sugar
2 teaspoons thin soy sauce
2 teaspoons thick soy sauce
2 teaspoons Shaohsing wine or
    medium-dry sherry
1½ teaspoons potato flour
2 tablespoons water
1 dried red chili, seeded and chopped
1 tablespoon hot chili oil (see page 240)

**For the sauce**
½ teaspoon potato flour
2 tablespoons water or clear stock
1 tablespoon thick soy sauce

**SERVES 4** with 2 other dishes

True to form, this Hunan dish is spicy hot, savory and slightly sweet. As if the flavors are not complex enough, tangy tangerine peel is added to provide a further dimension in taste. The orange rind is not a traditional ingredient for this dish, but it is used here because it complements rather than detracts from the tangerine peel.

**1**  Soak the tangerine peel in cold water for about 2 hours, or until soft. Drain and slice into strips about ⅕ inch (5 millimeters) wide.

**2**  Peel the orange rind lengthwise and blanch in boiling water for 5 minutes to remove its bitterness. Drain and rinse in cold water. Slice into strips similar to the tangerine strips.

**3**  Cut the beef into thickish slices, about 1 by 1½ inches (2.5 by 3.5 centimeters) and put into a bowl.

**4**  **Prepare the marinade:** Add the salt, sugar, soy sauces, wine or sherry and potato flour to the meat. Add the water, 1 tablespoon at a time, and stir in the same direction until all is absorbed. Mix in the chopped chili and let marinate for 30 to 60 minutes. Blend in the hot chili oil.

**5**  Heat a wok over high heat until smoke rises. Add the oil and swirl it around. Add the ginger, stir, then add the white scallions and let sizzle. Add the tangerine and orange peel and fry for a few seconds. Put in the beef and, sliding the wok scoop or metal spatula to the bottom of the wok, flip and turn for 1 or 2 minutes or until very hot. Splash in the wine or sherry around the side of the wok, continuing to stir. When the sizzling dies down, add the chili sauce. Cover, lower the heat and cook for about 2 minutes, so that the flavor of the tangerine peel can permeate the beef.

**6**  **Prepare the sauce:** Mix together the potato flour, water or stock and soy sauce.

**7**  Dribble into the wok and stir as the sauce thickens. Add the green scallions and stir to mix. Transfer to a warm serving dish. Serve immediately.

# Eight–treasure Vegetarian Assemblage

## INGREDIENTS

2 heaped tablespoons cloud ears, reconstituted (see page 33)

½ ounce (15 grams) golden needles, reconstituted (see page 33)

2 ounces (55 grams) cellophane noodles

1 teaspoon salt

4½ tablespoons peanut or corn oil

4 ounces (115 grams) sugar peas, trimmed

6 thin slices fresh ginger root, peeled

6 scallions, sliced diagonally

1 tablespoon fermented red bean curd cheese, mashed with 1 teaspoon own juice or water

8 bean curd puffs, halved (see page 24)

8 canned baby corn on the cob, halved lengthwise

4 ounces (115 grams) canned straw mushrooms

3 to 4 ounces (85 to 115 grams) canned ginkgo nuts

½ teaspoon sugar

2 to 2½ tablespoons thin soy sauce

6 ounces (175 grams) vegetable or clear stock mixed with ½ teaspoon potato flour

sesame oil to taste

**SERVES 6** with 3 other dishes

Eight is a significant number for the Chinese, for in Buddhism, which for many centuries exerted great influence in China, there are eight treasures in life: pearl, lozenge, stone chime, rhinoceros horn, coin, mirror, books and leaf. The symbolism of these eight treasures is not lost in Chinese food: any dish comprising eight or more main ingredients can term itself an "eight-treasure" dish.

**1** Drain the cloud ears and golden needles but leave damp. Break up the large pieces of cloud ears.

**2** Soak the cellophane noodles in plenty of boiling water for 30 minutes. They will expand and become pliable. Drain. Cut with scissors to shorten.

**3** Bring a saucepan of water to a boil and add ½ teaspoon of the salt and ½ tablespoon of the oil. Add the peas and, as soon as the water returns to a boil, drain in a colander. Refresh under cold running water and drain again.

**4** Heat a wok over high heat until smoke rises. Add the remaining oil and swirl it around. Add the ginger, then the scallions and stir for a few seconds. Add the red bean curd cheese and stir to blend. Add the cloud ears, toss and stir, then adjust the heat to moderate. Add the cellophane noodles, golden needles, bean curd puffs, baby corn, straw mushrooms and ginkgo nuts and mix together. Season with the remaining salt, sugar and soy sauce. Pour in the stock and cook, covered or uncovered, until much of the stock has been absorbed. Add the peas, mix well and heat through. Sprinkle with sesame oil to taste. Transfer to a warm serving dish. Serve hot.

# Stuffed Chinese Mushrooms

## INGREDIENTS

4 ounces (115 grams) pork shoulder
  or fresh ham
2 ounces (55 grams) canned bamboo
  shoots, or 3 or 4 fresh or canned water
  chestnuts, chopped fine
5 scallions, cut into tiny rounds
1 tablespoon peanut or corn oil
28 thick medium dried Chinese
  mushrooms, with slightly curled
  edges, reconstituted (see page 33)

**For the marinade**

2 to 4 thin slices fresh ginger root,
  peeled and finely minced
½ teaspoon salt
½ teaspoon sugar
2 teaspoons thin soy sauce
6 turns white pepper mill
1 teaspoon Shaohsing wine or
  medium-dry sherry
½ teaspoon potato flour
1 tablespoon water
1 tablespoon egg white

**For the sauce**

1½ teaspoons potato flour,
  dissolved in 1 tablespoon water
6 ounces (175 grams) mushroom water
1 tablespoon oyster sauce
1 tablespoon thick soy sauce
1½ to 2 tablespoons peanut or corn oil

**SERVES 6** with 3 or 4 other dishes

A delicately flavored steamed dish much enjoyed by the Cantonese and Fukienese. The egg white lightens the pork, and the bamboo shoots or water chestnuts add just a bite to the otherwise smooth texture. The sauce glistens on the stuffing, giving a transparent effect.

**1** Chop the pork by hand or mince coarsely. Put into a bowl.

**2 Prepare the marinade:** Add the ginger, salt, sugar, soy sauce, pepper, wine or sherry, potato flour and water to the pork. Stir vigorously for about 30 seconds, or until well coated. Add the egg white and stir again for another 30 seconds or until smooth and light. Let marinate for about 15 minutes.

**3** Mix the bamboo shoots or water chestnuts with the pork. Mix in the scallions. Stir in the 1 tablespoon of oil. The stuffing is now ready.

**4** Drain and squeeze out the excess water from the mushrooms but leave damp. Reserve the soaking liquid.

**5** Hold a mushroom cap in one hand with the hollow side up. Using a small knife, fill the hollow generously with stuffing, shaping it into a slightly sloping mound to give an attractive appearance. Repeat until all are done. Put on a heatproof dish, stuffing side up, preferably in one layer.

**6** Put the dish in a wok or steamer and steam, tightly covered, for 10 minutes over high heat (see page 43).

**7 Prepare the sauce:** A few minutes before the end of the steaming time, mix together the flour, mushroom water, oyster sauce and soy sauce. Pour into a wok or a saucepan. Bring to a boil, stirring continuously as it thickens. Blend in the oil, which will give a sheen.

**8** Remove the mushrooms from the steamer. Arrange them in 2 layers, either in the same heatproof dish or on a warm serving dish. Pour the sauce over them. Serve piping hot.

# Rainbow Salad

This multicolored plate of lightly stir-fried vegetables is made all the more delectable by the subtle dressing of sesame paste and vinegar. This dish can be prepared ahead of time and, if refrigerated, will keep overnight without losing much of its crunchiness.

**1** Drain and squeeze out excess water from the mushrooms but leave damp. Slice into the thinnest possible slivers.

**2** Cut the cucumber into very thin slices. Put into a bowl, sprinkle with ½ teaspoon of the salt to draw out excess water. Let stand for 15 to 30 minutes, then drain thoroughly.

**3** Cut the carrots into very thin slices. Put into a bowl, sprinkle with 1 teaspoon of salt to draw out excess water. Let stand for 15 to 30 minutes, then drain thoroughly.

**4** Slice the red pepper into thin strips.

**5 Prepare the dressing:** Mix the sesame paste with half of the water first and stir in the same direction; the paste will thicken. Add the rest of the water and continue to stir; the paste will become thinner. Now add the vinegar, little by little, stirring to blend. Stir in the salt and pepper.

**6** Heat a wok over high heat until smoke rises. Add 4 tablespoons of the oil and swirl it around. Add the white scallions and stir a couple of times. Stir in the mushrooms, then the red pepper and stir some more. Now add the carrots and bean sprouts. Sliding the wok scoop or metal spatula to the bottom of the wok, flip and turn vigorously over high heat for about 2 minutes, or until the vegetables are barely cooked and still very crunchy. Add the green scallions, stir a few more times and remove to a serving plate to cool. If water starts to ooze, drain.

**7** Heat a large frying pan over moderate heat. Add 1 tablespoon of oil, tipping the pan to ensure even spreading. When the oil is moderately hot, pour in the lightly beaten egg and quickly tip the pan to let the egg reach evenly to the edges. When cooked on one side, loosen the edges with a spatula and flip the crêpe over to cook the other side quickly, until firm but not hard. Transfer to a plate and cut into strips about 1½ inches (3.5 centimeters) long and ⅕ inch (5 millimeters) wide.

**8** When the stir-fried vegetables are cool, mix in the cucumber. Stir in the dressing and toss well. Arrange the egg strips on top.

**9** Chill, covered, in the refrigerator before serving. It can, however, be served at room temperature.

## INGREDIENTS

6 large dried Chinese mushrooms, reconstituted (see page 33)
12 ounces (350 grams) cucumber, halved lengthwise and seeded
1½ teaspoons salt
8 ounces (225 grams) carrots, peeled
1 medium red pepper, halved lengthwise and seeded
5 tablespoons groundnut or corn oil
7 scallions, halved lengthwise, cut into 2-inch (5-centimeter) sections, white and green parts separated
8 ounces (225 grams) bean sprouts
1 large egg, lightly beaten

**For the dressing**

2 tablespoons sesame paste
2 teaspoons water
4 or 5 teaspoons rice or white wine vinegar
½ teaspoon salt
10 turns pepper mill

**SERVES 4 TO 6** with 2 or 3 other dishes

# Lohan's Delight: Buddhist Vegetarian Dish

Lohan (monks or saints), following general Buddhist principles, were also known as "destroyers of the passions." Fittingly, this dish does not use any of the usual condiments—ginger, garlic and scallions—for in Buddhist belief they arouse human passions which, in turn, impede one's hopes of achieving Nirvana, the state of absolute peace and blessedness.

**1** Drain the cloud ears and golden needles and squeeze out excess water from the mushrooms, but leave damp. Reserve the mushroom soaking liquid.

**2** Soak the hair seaweed in plenty of cold or tepid water for about 10 minutes so that it will become pliable. Then rinse in many changes of water, picking it over, removing impurities and discarding the fine sand that settles at the bottom of the bowl.

**3 To cure:** Put the water, ginger, wine or sherry and oil in a wok or saucepan and bring to a boil. Submerge the seaweed and boil for about 5 minutes. Drain through a fine sieve and discard the ginger.

**4** Heat a wok over high heat until smoke rises. Add 1 tablespoon of the oil and swirl it around. Add the cloud ears and golden needles and toss and turn for about 30 seconds, adjusting the heat if the cloud ears make a loud explosive noise. Transfer to a warm dish nearby.

**5** Add the remaining oil and swirl it around. Add the mushrooms and bamboo shoots and turn and stir for about 30 seconds, or until very hot.

**6** Return the cloud ears and golden needles to the wok, and add the hair seaweed, ginkgo nuts and gluten pieces. Pour in the mushroom water, add the salt, sugar and soy sauce and bring to a boil. Cover, lower the heat and simmer fast for 10 to 15 minutes, or until most of the water has been absorbed.

**7** Transfer to a warm serving plate. Sprinkle on the sesame oil and serve.

# Plain Fried Rice

## INGREDIENTS

3 cups or 14 ounces boiled rice, cooked
  at least 3 or 4 hours in advance (see
  page 170)
2 tablespoons peanut or corn oil
2 scallions, cut into small rounds, white
  and green parts separated
1 large egg, lightly beaten with
  2 teaspoons oil and ¼ teaspoon salt
¼ teaspoon salt or to taste
2 teaspoons thick soy sauce
2 tablespoons clear stock (optional)

**SERVES 2** with 1 other dish

When cooked rice is stir-fried with egg but without meat or seafood, it is called "plain fried rice," and it often has greater appeal than boiled rice to those who are not used to eating rice as a staple. The stir-frying process adds much taste and fragrance. The Chinese sometimes serve it in place of boiled rice as a measure of economy when there are few dishes to go with it. Since the best result is obtained from cooked rice that has been left for a few hours or overnight, it is also a way to turn any leftover rice into an appetizing dish.

**1** Loosen the rice grains as much as possible.

**2** Heat a wok over high heat until smoke rises. Add the oil and swirl it around. Add the white scallions, stir a few times, then pour in the egg. Let stand for 5 to 10 seconds, so that the egg sets at the bottom but remains runny on the surface.

**3** Add the rice. Sliding the wok scoop or metal spatula to the bottom of the wok, turn and toss continuously for 3 or 4 minutes or until thoroughly hot. Season with the salt and soy sauce. If the rice is very hard, add the stock and stir for a few more seconds. Add the green scallions. Put in a warm serving bowl and serve immediately.

# Dry-braised Yi Noodles

## INGREDIENTS

2 Yi noodle cakes, 8 ounces (225 grams),
 each cake is usually 10 inches
 (25 centimeters) in diameter)
1 ounce (25 grams) dried shrimp, rinsed
3½ tablespoons peanut or corn oil
3 cloves garlic, peeled and chopped fine
¼ inch (5 millimeters) fresh ginger root,
 peeled and chopped fine
8 ounces (225 grams) cooked
 white crabmeat
¼ teaspoon salt
1½ to 2 cups prime or clear stock
 (see page 242)
6 scallions, sliced into 2-inch
 (5-centimeter) sections and cut
 into silken threads (see page 34)
½ tablespoon thin soy sauce
3 tablespoons oyster sauce

**SERVES 8** as the last dish to
end a dinner of 5 or 6 dishes

Called in China "Noodles of the Yi mansion," this dish is believed to have
been invented by the scholar-official Yi Ping-shou, in the 18th century. Yi,
who had a gourmet's palate for noodles, wanted them kneaded only with
egg, no water, then deep-fried before being braised in the best stock. The
Yi noodle cakes sold in Chinese stores are already deep-fried.

**1** Put 7 to 8 cups of water in a large saucepan and bring to a boil. Break each
noodle cake into 3 or 4 pieces and submerge them in the water. Return to a boil
and continue to boil for about 1 minute, or until the noodles are tender but not
soggy. Drain in a colander and set aside. (If prepared several hours in advance,
rinse under cold running water.)

**2** Soak the shrimp for about 15 minutes in just enough boiling water to cover
them. Drain them, reserving the soaking liquid. Chop the shrimp into pieces the
size of matchstick heads.

**3** Heat a wok over high heat until smoke rises. Add ½ tablespoon of the oil
and swirl it around. Add the shrimp, toss and stir for 1 or 2 minutes, or until dry.
Transfer to a small dish.

**4** Rinse and dry the wok and reheat over high heat until smoke rises. Add the
remaining oil and swirl it around. Add the garlic, and when it takes on color, add
the ginger and stir a few times. Add the crabmeat and stir with the wok scoop
or metal spatula. Season with the salt.

**5** Pour in the stock and bring to a boil. Add the noodles, mix with the crab
meat and continue to cook over moderate heat until most of the stock has
been absorbed. Add the scallions, season with the soy sauce and oyster sauce,
and check for taste.

**6** Transfer to a warm serving dish. Sprinkle the shrimp on top and serve.

**Note:** Leftover noodles reheat well when a little stock is added to them.

# Singapore Fried Rice Sticks

It is always interesting to note how cuisines influence each other. When the Fukienese emigrated to Singapore during the 19th century they took with them one of their favorite dishes: Fried rice sticks. As time went by, curry spices were added, to suit local taste, and they remain a distinctive element now that the dish has been readopted by the Southern Chinese.

## INGREDIENTS

4 ounces (115 grams) fresh or frozen
 raw shrimp or prawns, shelled
6 ounces (175 grams) dried rice sticks
½ cup peanut or corn oil
1 egg, lightly beaten
1 small onion, skinned and
 shredded lengthwise
1 small green pepper, seeded and
 cut into matchstick-sized pieces
4 ounces (115 grams) char-siu
 (Cantonese roast pork, see page 138),
 cut into matchstick-sized pieces
1 teaspoon curry powder

**For the marinade**
⅕ teaspoon salt
½ teaspoon cornstarch
1 tablespoon egg white

**For the sauce**
¼ cup clear stock or water
¾ teaspoon salt
½ teaspoon sugar
1 tablespoon thin soy sauce

**SERVES 3 OR 4** as a snack

**1** If frozen shrimp are used, defrost thoroughly, then pat dry. Put into a bowl. If prawns are used, devein and quarter.

**2  Prepare the marinade:** Add the salt and cornstarch to the shrimp and stir to mix. Add the egg white and stir vigorously in the same direction until the shrimp are well coated. Let marinate for 2 or 3 hours in the refrigerator.

**3** Submerge the rice sticks in sufficiently hot but not boiling water to cover them completely. Soak for about 30 minutes, until soft and pliable. Drain. Make several cuts with scissors to shorten their length so that they can be handled more easily.

**4  Prepare the sauce:** Mix together the stock or water, salt, sugar and soy sauce.

**5** Heat a flat frying pan until hot. Add 1 tablespoon of the oil and swirl it to the edges. Turn the heat down, pour in the egg and, tilting the pan, spread it to the edges to make a crêpe. As soon as it is set, turn it over, fry the other side for a few seconds and transfer to a plate. Slice into narrow strips about 2 inches (5 centimeters) long.

**6** Heat a wok over high heat until smoke rises. Add 4 tablespoons of the oil and swirl it around. Add the onion and turn and stir for about 30 seconds. Add the shrimp and toss and turn in rapid succession for about 1 minute, or until cooked and turning pinkish. Scoop onto a dish, leaving as much oil behind as possible.

**7** Tip the green pepper into the wok and stir for about 30 seconds. Add the char-siu and stir together for another minute, or until piping hot. Scoop onto a dish.

**8** Add another 4 tablespoons of the oil to the wok and swirl it around. Add the curry powder and let it sizzle for a few seconds. Add the rice sticks and sauce. Holding 2 pairs of chopsticks or 2 large wooden spoons, lift and toss the rice sticks until they have absorbed almost all the sauce. Add the remaining oil around the side of the wok to prevent the rice sticks from sticking. Taste, and if they are hard rather than *al dente*, add 2 or 3 tablespoons of stock or water and cook for 1 or 2 minutes over low heat with the wok cover on. Return the onion, shrimp, green pepper, char-siu and egg to the wok, toss and mix with the rice sticks. Remove to a warm serving dish. Serve immediately.

# Almond Bean Curd

## INGREDIENTS

3½ cups water
about 8 heaped tablespoons
  or ¼ ounce (10 grams) cut-up agar
5 tablespoons sugar
¾ cup evaporated milk
1 tablespoon almond essence
1 large can lychees

**SERVES 6**

In cookery, the Chinese often enjoy making up a dish to resemble the looks, if not also the taste, of a particular ingredient and giving the dish the same name. This very light and delightful summer dessert that looks like bean curd is, in fact, not bean curd at all!

**1** Put the water in a saucepan and bring to a boil. Add the agar, reduce the heat and simmer, to dissolve, for 20 to 25 minutes, stirring occasionally.

**2** Add the sugar and stir until completely dissolved.

**3** Remove the saucepan from the heat. Pour in the evaporated milk and stir once.

**4** Strain the mixture through a fine sieve into a serving bowl, discarding any dregs from the agar.

**5** Stir in the almond essence. Let cool and set, then put into the refrigerator to chill.

**6** Cut the "bean curd" into diamond-shaped pieces. Put into a dish and top with lychees. Serve cold.

**Note:** Other fruits, fresh or canned, such as kiwi, peaches, grapes, pineapple, mangoes, can also be used. Instead of agar, about 6 level teaspoons of powdered gelatin can be used.

# Apples or Bananas Pulling Golden Threads

## INGREDIENTS

3 apples, Granny Smith or Golden
   Delicious or 3 fairly large bananas,
   on the unripe side
1 tablespoon all-purpose flour
peanut or corn oil for deep-frying
6 tablespoons fresh peanut or corn oil
9 tablespoons sugar
1 heaped teaspoon white sesame seeds

**For the batter**
4 ounces (115 grams) self-rising flour
1 large egg, lightly beaten
about 8 tablespoons water
1 tablespoon peanut or corn oil

**SERVES 6 TO 8**

In this recipe, an ingenious and foolproof Chinese method of caramelizing sugar in a few tablespoonfuls of hot oil is used in the preparation of this delicious dessert. What's more, the oil is then separated from the caramel and can be reused for other cooking.

**1  Prepare the batter:** Sift the flour into a mixing bowl and stir in the egg. Add the water gradually and stir to blend into a smooth batter, like thick cream in consistency. Let stand for about 15 minutes, then blend in the oil.

**2**  Peel and core the apples or peel the bananas and remove any strings. Divide each apple or roll cut each banana into 8 pieces (see page 33). Sprinkle on the all-purpose flour and toss well to mix.

**3**  Half fill a wok or deep fryer with oil. Heat to a temperature of 350°F (180°C), or until a cube of stale bread browns in 60 seconds. One by one, dip the fruit pieces into the batter. Add to the oil and deep-fry for about 2 or 3 minutes, or until pale golden. Remove with a pair of chopsticks or perforated spoon and drain on paper towels. (This can be done several hours in advance.) Reheat the oil to the same temperature. Deep-fry the fruits for a second time for about 1 minute, or until crisp and golden in color. Remove with a hand strainer or perforated spoon and drain on paper towels.

**4**  Fill a large bowl with water, add some ice cubes. Set aside.

**5**  Heat a well-cleaned and salt-free wok or heavy saucepan over high heat. Add the fresh oil, swirl it around and heat until smoke rises. Add the sugar and let it dissolve in the oil over moderately high heat, stirring all the time (a). Almost as soon as the sugar has completely dissolved, it will turn light brown in color. Immediately add all the fruit pieces (b) and sprinkle on the sesame seeds (c). Using two wok scoops or

# Regional Chinese Cooking

China is a vast country and as such is exposed to extremes of both geography and climate. This naturally results in the growth of different agricultural products, so it is little wonder that cuisines vary from province to province. Even though there has never been agreement on the subject, many cookbooks divide Chinese cuisines into eight main streams: Peking, Shantung, Kiangsu, Anhwei, Kwangtung, Fukien, Szechwan and Hunan; others analyze the subregional cuisines within some of these provinces. However, I follow the practice of broadly carving the Chinese gastronomic map into four main regions: Peking or Northern, Shanghai or Eastern, Canton or Southern and Szechwan or Western.

One may well ask what constitutes regional differences, since there are basic national characteristics underlining all of the regional cuisines. The main cooking methods—boiling, steaming, braising, sautéing, deep-frying and stir-frying—are used by all Chinese, the wok is the national cooking utensil, and soy sauce is a ubiquitous and indispensable seasoning. The differences are subtle, and are related to climate, to local produce, to the mixing and use of different condiments, to the emphasis on a certain technique and to the manner of presentation.

## Peking or Northern cuisine

This is the largest area, embracing Inner Mongolia, Hopei, Honan, Shantung, Shansi and Shensi provinces. Although Shantung has a more temperate climate, the overall climate of the area is very harsh; Peking itself suffers from extreme heat in the summer and extreme cold in the winter, and in the spring suffers from periodic sandstorms, blown in from the Gobi Desert.

Wheat, millet, sorghum, peanuts, corn and soybeans are the main crops and Tientsin cabbage, better known as Chinese leaf or Chinese celery cabbage, cucumber, and celery are the main vegetables grown. Noodles, steamed breads and buns are a more popular staple than rice, and, unlike the Southern Chinese, who habitually eat their noodles in soup, Northern Chinese eat them on the dry side, seasoned with a sauce.

Food from Inner Mongolia and Shantung forms the backbone of Northern cuisine. The Mongolian influence is reflected in the many lamb dishes eaten, the most famous of which are Mongolian fire pot and lamb slices barbecued on a spit. In fact, mutton here is eaten and cooked in more ways than in any other region in China. Besides bringing refined dishes to the capital, Shantung chefs left their imprint on Peking cuisine with their liking for raw garlic and leeks.

Peking cuisine may be considered plain and robust, but since the 19th century it has exported one dish that has captivated the imagination of the whole world: Peking duck. The duck is fattened specially for the table, roasted in a special oven, then pancakes and a special sauce are made to accompany it. In Peking, the duck can be an all-in-one meal, in which the head, tongue and feet are served as separate courses alongside the more familiar crispy skin and meat.

## Shanghai or Eastern cuisine

This area, based around the Yangtze delta and covering Kiangsu, Chekiang and Anhwei provinces, is temperate in climate and its fertile land, traversed by many rivers and ponds, is a rich agricultural area growing both wheat and rice, and yielding much fish and seafood.

Taken as a whole, Eastern cuisine is rich, decorative and rather on the sweet side; unlike Peking food, garlic is used sparingly, if at all. Although Shanghai is the name used to identify the Eastern school, there are other culinary centers, represented by the main cities of the area—Hangchow, Yangchow, Suchow and Wuhsi, for example. The area as a whole is renowned for certain products and dishes: the specially cured Chinhua ham, with its pinkish red flesh and succulently savory-sweet taste, the rich dark Chinkiang vinegar and the amber-coloured Shaohsing rice wine. Classic dishes include Crisp stir-fried shrimp, Eel cooked in oil, Yangchow fried rice, Lion's head and fish from the West Lake with a sweet and sour sauce.

One special cooking technique of the region has been adopted nationally. This is *hung-shao*, or the red-braising method of cooking, whereby the ingredients (mainly meat, poultry and fish) are cooked slowly in an aromatic mixture of thick dark soy sauce and rice wine. When, at the end of cooking, the sauce is reduced and spooned over the main ingredient, the resulting taste is both rich and fragrant.

Shanghai cuisine is the least known outside China. Its oiliness and sweetness are perhaps less appealing to the Western palate, and because it is decorative, it tends to be labor-intensive. Moreover, it depends largely on fresh local produce; the famous Shanghai crabs, studded with yellow roe in the autumn, have no counterpart elsewhere, and for the delicate taste of the famous West Lake fish one *has* to go to Hangchow.

## Szechwan or Western cuisine

Western cuisine is represented by the provinces of Szechwan, Hunan and Yunnan, and of these Szechwan is the most influential. A land of precipitous mountains and the Yangtze gorges, and home of the pandas, Szechwan is the most populous province in China. Fortunately it is also known as one of China's rice bowls. Very humid and rainy in the summer but mild in the winter, the temperate climate is suitable for agricultural growth almost all year round. With good irrigation, the Szechwan basin in the east of the province grows rice, wheat, rapeseed, corn and bamboo shoots; citrus fruits, especially tangerines, and mushrooms are also grown. A spice, Szechwan peppercorns, and a preserved vegetable are two special products.

Many people, when they first encounter Szechwan food, find it highly seasoned and spicily hot. Fresh and dried red chili are evident, providing the fiery result. But, in fact, the sophistication of Szechwan cooking goes far beyond this apparent overspicIness. Often in the same dish, the full spectrum of tastes can be experienced: salty, sweet, vinegary and hot. Rather than overpowering the taste buds, the Szechwanese claim that the chili pepper is only a harbinger awakening them, and that once stimulated, they will be able to appreciate the full range of tastes and aftertastes.

Special Szechwanese dishes are Hot and sour soup, Fragrant and crispy duck, Twice-cooked pork and a range of fish fragrant dishes.

In terms of cookery techniques, Szechwan dishes often employ multiple processes; for example, its famous smoked duck, which is first marinated, then smoked, steamed and finally deep-fried.

## Cantonese or Southern cuisine

The climate of the area centered in the provinces of Kwantung and Fukien is subtropical, with heavy rainfalls between May and September; the coast is subject to typhoons. The Pearl River delta of Kwangtung and the coastal plains of Fukien are rich agricultural areas. Rice crops are harvested twice a year, and rice is the staple, eaten twice a day. Sweet potato, corn, taro and wheat are also cultivated. There are many pig and poultry farms, and fish ponds. Vegetables, especially green leafy vegetables, abound. Tropical fruits, oranges, bananas, peaches, pineapples and juicy lychees are plentiful. High-quality tea is a special product of Fukien, while all along the coast fish and seafood—crabs, crayfish, shrimps, prawns, scallops, clams—are plentiful. This wealth of ingredients has helped to make Cantonese cooking the most versatile and varied of Chinese cuisines.

Cantonese food is not highly seasoned. Instead, a harmonious blending of different flavors is sought in order to bring out the best of the ingredients. However, this does mean that it often relies upon fresh ingredients and when they are not available and substitutes have to be used the results can taste insipid.

Although they are adept at all Chinese culinary techniques, Cantonese cooks are at their most skillful when they stir-fry dishes. Red-braised dishes are an Eastern contribution to Chinese gastronomy, but Southern stir-fried dishes reign supreme nationwide. Their "wok-fragrance," a term used to describe the aroma so desirable in stir-fried dishes, is matchless.

Dim sum—hot hors d'oeuvres of pastry cases stuffed with a mixture of delicacies such as pork, beef or seafood, bamboo shoots or mushroom, steamed, sautéed or deep-fried—is another Cantonese speciality. There are, of course, dim sum in all the other regional cuisines, but none can beat the Cantonese for variety. Because of the time, labor and special skill called for to make dim sum, they are a treat to be enjoyed at restaurants more than at home.

MAP OF COOKING
REGIONS OF CHINA

INNER MONGOLIA
Hu-ho-hao-t'e
Beijing (formerly Peking)
Tientsin
HOPEH
Yin-ch'uan
T'ai-yüan
Chi-nan
Yellow Sea
Lan-chou
SHANSI
SHANTUNG
Cheng-chou
Hsi-an
HONAN
KIANGSU
SHENSI
Nan-ching
Yang-chow
Pacific Ocean
SZECHWAN
HUPEH
Ho-fei
Shanghai
Ch'eng-tu
Wu-han
ANHWEI
Ch'ung-ch'ing
Nan-ch'ang
Hang-chow
Shaohsing
Chinhua
CHEKIANG
Ch'ang-sha
KIANGSI
FUKIEN
KWEICHOW
HUNAN
Fu-chou
Kuei-yang
Hsia-men (Amoy)
K'un-ming
T'ai-pei
YUNNAN
KWANGSI
KWANGTUNG
Nan-ning
Canton
TAIWAN
HONG KONG

COOKING REGIONS
- Western/Szechwan
- Southern/Canton
- Northern/Peking
- Eastern/Shanghai

# A Northern or Peking Menu

The main feature of this menu for six is, without doubt, the Peking duck, with its pancake accompaniment. In fact, they alone, with any one of the other dishes, should make four people feel well fed and contented.

# Key

# Mandarin Pancakes

## INGREDIENTS

1 pound (450 grams) all-purpose flour
1½ cups boiling water
1 tablespoon cold water
little extra flour
2 teaspoons sesame oil

**SERVES 6** with Peking duck

Mandarin pancakes are a must with Peking duck, but they are also traditionally served with dishes such as Mu-shu pork (see page 140). The Northern Chinese like these pancakes to be slightly on the firm side; the little bit of cold water added to the dough does the trick.

**1** Sift the flour into a mixing bowl. Pour in the boiling water gradually, stirring vigorously with a wooden spoon or a pair of chopsticks until well mixed. Then stir in the cold water. As soon as your hands can withstand the heat, form the mixture into a dough and knead lightly either in the bowl or on a lightly floured board, or work surface for 3 or 4 minutes or until soft and smooth. Allow to stand in the bowl for 20 to 30 minutes covered with a cloth.

**2** Transfer the dough to a lightly floured board or work surface. Divide into 2 equal portions and knead a few more times, until smooth again. Use as little extra flour on the board as possible or the pancakes will taste floury.

**3** Using both hands, roll each portion of dough into a roll 16 inches (40 centimeters) long. Then, using a ruler as a guide, divide each roll into 1-inch (2.5-centimeter) pieces (a), making a total of 32.

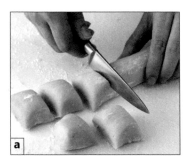

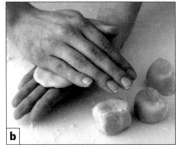

**4** One by one, stand each piece upright on the heel of your hand, slightly round off the dough, then flatten with the other hand (b), into a circle of about 2 to 2½ inches (5 to 6 centimeters) diameter.

**5** Using a brush, paint the surface of half of the pieces (16) with sesame oil (c). Place the remaining pieces on the oiled surfaces (d), making 16 pairs. Shape each pair of circles as evenly as possible.

**6** Using a lightly floured rolling pin, roll out each pair into thin pancakes about 6 to 6½ inches (15 to 16 centimeters) in diameter (e). To ensure even thickness and roundness, rotate the circles quite frequently, turning them over as well.

**7** Heat an unoiled, flat heavy frying pan or griddle over medium-to-low heat. Put in 1 pair of cakes at a time and fry for 1 or 2 minutes, or until light brown spots appear (f). Turn over to fry the other side. In less than 1 minute part of the surface will puff up, indicating that they are done.

**8** Remove from the frying pan, and while they are still hot separate the 2 thin pancakes with the fingers (g). Put on a plate and cover with a cloth to prevent drying. Repeat until all are done.

**9** Steam all the pancakes (in 2 batches, if necessary) in a wok or steamer for 5 to 10 minutes before serving (see page 43).

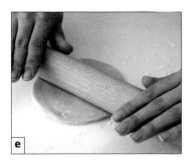

# An Eastern or Shanghai Menu

This menu for eight reflects the cuisines of the two Eastern gastronomic provinces: Kiangsu and Chekiang. Between them, they boast of several of the best products in China: Chinhua ham, Shaohsing wine and Chinkiang vinegar. In this menu, the decorative and delicate dishes are balanced by more down-to-earth dishes.

## Key

1. **Fu-yung egg slices**
   Tender pieces of egg served in a nourishing and tasty stock (see page 210).

2. **Red-in-snow soup with pork**
   Tasty soup with pork, cellophane noodles and crisp red-in-snow as main ingredients (see page 208).

3. **Yangchow fried rice**
   Fried rice cooked with ham, shrimp, peas and onions, garnished with strips of egg (see page 213).

4. **"Smoked" fish Shanghai style**
   Cold dish, marinated, deep-fried then steeped in a tangy sauce (see page 209).

5. **Eight-treasure bean curd**
   Savory dish of puréed bean curd flavored with chicken, ham, mushrooms and nuts (see page 212).

6. **Crystal sugar pig's hock**
   Tender meat dish, spiced with ginger, scallions, soy sauce and wine, served whole (see page 211).

**8** Using an unserrated table knife, make a crisscross pattern on each semicircle (b). Then, using the blunt side of the knife, make 2 indentations, ½ inch (1 centimeter) deep, along the edge (c).

**9** Space the buns out in one layer on a very wet cloth on a steaming rack. Steam in a wok or steamer over high heat for about 12 minutes (see page 43). Remove from the heat.

**10** Transfer the buns to a wire rack for a few seconds, then put on a warm plate and serve.

# Silver Thread Buns

## INGREDIENTS

¾ teaspoon dried yeast
2 teaspoons sugar
1 cup tepid water
3¾ cups all-purpose flour
3½ ounces (100 grams) lard
little extra flour
2½ tablespoons sugar

**MAKES ABOUT 18 TO 20 BUNS**

**1** Put the dried yeast and sugar in a small bowl, add the water and stir. Leave in a warm place until the yeast froths on the surface.

**2** Sift the flour into a mixing bowl. Rub in 1 tablespoon of the lard with the fingertips. Stir in the yeast liquid and work it into a dough. Knead lightly for 1 or 2 minutes, until the dough is smooth. Either cover the dough with a damp cloth or cover the bowl with plastic wrap. Let stand in a warm place for at least 1 hour, so that the dough will rise to more than double in size.

**3** Cream the remaining lard and sugar until well blended.

**4** Knead the risen dough on a lightly floured board for a few seconds, until smooth.

**5** Roll out the dough with a lightly floured rolling pin into a thin circular or oblong sheet about 20 inches (50 centimeters) across. Spread evenly with the sugar-and-lard mixture, using a broad knife. Fold the sheet over and over at 3-inch (7.5-centimeter) intervals. Slice crosswise into thin "silver" threads about ⅛ inch (3 millimeters) wide (a).

**6** Group 7 or 8 strings of silver threads together and, using both hands, pull them slowly across into a rope 12 inches (30 centimeters) long (b).

**7** Lay the rope on the floured board, turn one end away from you (c), and roll toward the other end to make a spiral tower, the base being about 2 inches (5 centimeters) in diameter. Repeat until all are done.

**8** Space them out in one layer on a very wet cloth on a steaming rack (d). Steam in a wok or steamer over high heat for 15 minutes (see page 43). Transfer the buns to a wire rack for a few seconds, then put on a warm plate and serve.

# A Southern or Cantonese Menu

Cantonese and Fukienese cuisines, the two distinctive representatives of the Southern region, specialize in seafood. Hence this predominantly seafood menu for eight. However, for those less fond of seafood there are more than enough classic meat and poultry dishes from the south from which to choose.

# Key

# Clear–steamed Sea Bass

The sea bass and the striped bass are arguably the most popular fish for Chinese living in Europe and America. Not surprisingly, they serve them steamed.

### INGREDIENTS

1 sea bass, 1½ to 2½ pounds
  (675 grams to 1.15 kilograms),
  cleaned with head left on
¼ teaspoon salt
¼ teaspoon sugar
½ to ¾ inch (1 to 2 centimeters) fresh
  ginger root, peeled and cut into silken
  threads (see page 35)
5 to 7 scallions cut into 2-inch
  (5-centimeter) sections and then
  silken threads (see page 34), green
  and white parts separated
4 or 5 tablespoons peanut or corn oil
2 or 3 tablespoons thin soy sauce

**SERVES 2** as a main course;
4 to 6 with 2 or 3 other dishes

**1** Pat the fish dry. Make 2 or 3 diagonal slashes on both sides of the fish. Lay it on a heatproof serving dish with slightly raised sides. If your wok or steamer is rather small, the fish can be halved.

**2** Steam in a wok or steamer over high heat for about 8 minutes, until the fish is cooked and the flesh flakes easily (see page 43). Remove the cover, reduce the heat or turn it off. If too much water from the steam has collected on the dish, use paper towels to absorb some of it.

**3** Sprinkle with the salt and sugar. Spread the ginger, then the green, and finally the white scallions on the fish.

**4** Heat the oil in a small saucepan over high heat until smoke rises. Pour it, little by little, over the scallions and ginger. The sizzling oil partially cooks them, enhancing the flavor.

**5** Remove the dish from the wok or steamer. Add the soy sauce and serve immediately.

# Stir-fried Fillet of Beef with Mango

This sophisticated modern dish is especially popular in the South of China where mangoes are greatly enjoyed. The combination of the sharpness of the ginger, the natural sweetness of the mango and the savory sauce makes the beef an intriguing proposition to the palate.

**1** Cut the fillet across the grain into chunky strips, about 2 inches (5 centimeters) long and ½ inch (1 centimeter) thick. Beat the beef strips with the broad side of a cleaver to loosen the fibers. Put into a bowl.

**2 Prepare the marinade:** Add the salt, sugar, soy sauces, wine or sherry and pepper to the beef. Sprinkle with the potato flour, add the water, 1 tablespoon at a time, and stir vigorously to coat the pieces well. Let marinate in the refrigerator for 20 to 30 minutes.

**3** Peel the mango, slice the flesh from the stone and then cut into strips.

**4 Prepare the sauce:** Mix together the potato flour, oyster sauce, soy sauce and water in a cup and put aside.

**5** Half fill a wok or deep fryer with oil. Heat to a temperature of 350°F (180°C), or until a cube of stale bread browns in 60 seconds. Tip the beef into the oil and, using a long pair of chopsticks or a wooden spoon, stir gently to make sure that all the pieces "go through the oil" for about 30 seconds, to have their juices sealed in. Transfer them at once to a warm plate with a large hand strainer.

**6** Empty all but 3 tablespoons of the oil into a container and reserve for other use.

**7** Reheat the oil over high heat until smoke rises. Add the garlic, which will sizzle and take on color. Add the white scallions, stirring, and then add the ginger. Now return the beef to the wok and turn and toss with the wok scoop or metal spatula for about 30 seconds. Splash in the wine or sherry around the side of the wok. If you like your beef underdone, remove once the sizzling has died down. If you prefer your beef well done, leave to cook a little longer, stirring until done. Keep warm.

**8** Add up to 1 tablespoon of oil to the wok, swirl it around and add the mango. Cover and fry over a gentle heat for about 1 minute.

**9** Add the well-stirred sauce to the wok. When it thickens and bubbles, add the green scallions. Attractively arrange the mango, green scallions and sauce with the beef. Serve immediately.

## INGREDIENTS

1 pound (450 grams) beef fillet, trimmed
1 large mango, not too ripe
peanut or corn oil for deep-frying
4 cloves garlic, peeled and chopped fine
4 scallions, cut into 1-inch
   (2.5-centimeter) sections,
   white and green parts separated
¾ inch (2 centimeters) fresh ginger root,
   cut into silken threads (see page 35)
1 tablespoon Shaohsing wine or
   medium-dry sherry

**For the marinade**
¼ teaspoon salt
½ teaspoon sugar
1 teaspoon thin soy sauce
1 teaspoon thick soy sauce
1 teaspoon Shaohsing wine or
   medium-dry sherry
4 turns black pepper mill
1½ teaspoons potato flour
2 tablespoons water

**For the sauce**
½ teaspoon potato flour
2 teaspoons oyster sauce
1 teaspoon thin soy sauce
3 tablespoons water

**SERVES 4 with 2 other dishes**

# Dry-fried Prawns

## INGREDIENTS

1½ pounds (675 grams) fresh or frozen
    medium raw prawns in the shell,
    without heads
¾ teaspoon sea salt
peanut or corn oil
4 cloves garlic, peeled and chopped fine
½ to ¾ inch (1 to 2 centimeters) fresh
    ginger root, peeled and chopped fine
2 fresh green chilies, seeded and chopped
4 large scallions, cut into small rounds,
    white and green parts separated

**For the sauce**
⅛ teaspoon potato flour
2 tablespoons thin soy sauce
2 teaspoons sugar
1 tablespoon Shaohsing wine or
    medium-dry sherry
1 tablespoon ketchup

**SERVES 6 TO 8** with 3 or 4 other dishes

This dish traditionally calls for large prawns, but I have adapted it
to medium-sized ones.

**1** If frozen prawns are used, defrost thoroughly. Wash the shells well and
remove the legs. Devein, if preferred, although there is no harm in not doing
so (see page 99). Pat dry with paper towels. Put into a large bowl.

**2** Sprinkle with the salt and mix well. Let stand for about 20 minutes.

**3 Prepare the sauce:** Mix together the potato flour, soy sauce, sugar,
wine or sherry and ketchup.

**4** Half fill a wok or deep fryer with oil. Heat to a temperature of 350°F (180°C),
or until a cube of stale bread browns in 60 seconds. Tip in all the prawns, "to go
through the oil" for about 30 seconds, moving them gently with either long
bamboo chopsticks or a wooden spoon. Turn off the heat, remove immediately
with a large hand strainer and drain on paper towels. The prawns, now pinkish,
will be almost cooked.

**5** Empty all but 2 or 3 tablespoons of oil into another container and keep
for future use.

**6** Reheat the oil in a wok until smoke rises. Add the garlic, stir a couple of
times, then the ginger, stir, then the chili, stir, and then the white scallions and
stir a few more times. Return the prawns to the wok and spread them out into
a single layer, if possible. Lower the heat and sauté the prawns for about 30
seconds, letting them absorb the aroma of the garlic and ginger. Turn them
over and sauté for another 30 seconds, taking care not to burn them.

**7** Pour the well-stirred sauce over the prawns. As you do so, turn and toss
the prawns with a wok scoop or metal spatula until most of the sauce has
been absorbed. Add the green scallions, transfer to a warm serving platter
and serve immediately.

**8** To eat, pick up one prawn with a pair of chopsticks, bite into it and shell
it with your front teeth while savoring the sauce on the shell. Neatly spit
the shell onto a side plate and eat the prawn meat in the normal way. If
you want an easier way of eating the prawns, I suggest you use your fingers.

# Red Bean Fool

It is not the Chinese custom to serve a dessert after each meal; fruit is served instead. However, this inexpensive pudding is very popular with the Cantonese; it has a thickish consistency and is not overly sweet. They serve it hot, without cream.

**1** Soak the beans and rice for half a day or overnight in 5 cups of cold water. Do not drain. (This step may be omitted.)

**2** Put the beans, rice and peel into a large saucepan, add the oil and the remaining cold water. If step 1 has been omitted, add all the cold water. Bring to a boil. (If boiling water is poured on the tangerine peel, it will taste bitter.) Lower the heat, cover and simmer for 2 hours, stirring occasionally and checking the water level. The volume should be reduced to 4 to 4½ cups for the right consistency—gluey—with water just covering the beans.

**3** Add the sugar and simmer until completely dissolved. Remove and discard the tangerine peel. Leave uncovered to cool.

**4** Liquidize the bean mixture. Chill the fool in the refrigerator. Serve, with cream, at the table.

**Note:** For those who like a more pronounced flavor of the tangerine peel, it can be liquidized with the cooked red beans. Also try the fool served hot with cream.

## INGREDIENTS

8 ounces (225 grams) red beans (azuki beans), washed and drained
4 teaspoons glutinous rice, washed and drained
6 cups cold water
1 piece dried tangerine peel, washed
3 teaspoons peanut or corn oil
1 cup sugar
heavy cream to serve (optional)

**SERVES 6**

# A Mixed Regional Menu

In planning your own menus, I urge you to mix the different regional dishes so that you can get the full benefit of the various tastes and flavors from the four corners of China. This menu for eight should be but a starting point for you.

# Key

# Yu-ling's Hot and Numbing Chicken

## INGREDIENTS

2 chicken breasts, about 1 pound 2 ounces
   to 1 pound 4 ounces (500 or 550 grams),
   skinned and boned
peanut or corn oil
1 teaspoon Szechwan peppercorns
2 large cloves garlic, peeled and sliced
4 thin slices fresh ginger
1 large scallion, cut into 1½-inch
   (3.5-centimeter) sections
2 or 3 fresh green chilies, each about
   3 inches (7.5 centimeters) long, seeded
   and sliced diagonally into long strips
1 tablespoon Shaohsing wine
   or medium-dry sherry
¼ teaspoon salt
¼ to ½ teaspoon sugar
½ teaspoon ground roasted
   Szechwan peppercorns
½ teaspoon cornstarch dissolved
   in 2 tablespoons water
1 teaspoon sesame oil

**For the marinade**
½ teaspoon salt
6 turns white pepper mill
1 teaspoon cornstarch
½ egg white, lightly beaten

**SERVES 4** with 2 other dishes

Chiang Yu-ling, my Mandarin teacher and friend, herself an excellent cook of Northern cuisine, has contributed much interest and information to this book. She has kindly given me this recipe.

**1** Cut the chicken into large cubes. Put into a bowl.

**2 Prepare the marinade:** Add the salt, pepper, cornstarch and egg white to the chicken. Stir in the same direction until well coated. Let marinate for 20 to 30 minutes.

**3** Half fill a wok or deep fryer with oil. Heat until it is just hot (about 225°F [110°C]). Add the chicken to "go through the oil" for about 60 to 75 seconds, separating the pieces with a long pair of chopsticks. Remove with a large hand strainer or perforated spoon and keep nearby. The chicken, having turned whitish, will be almost cooked.

**4** Empty all but 2 tablespoons of the oil into a container and save for other uses. Reheat the oil over medium heat. Add the Szechwan peppercorns and fry for about 1 minute, or until they have released their aroma and turned dark brown. Remove and discard.

**5** Add the garlic, ginger and scallion and fry over high heat until the edges are brown and their aroma released. Remove and discard.

**6** Lower the heat and add the chilies. Stir and turn for about 1 minute to release their peppery hot flavor, taking care not to burn them. Transfer to a small dish and keep nearby.

**7** Turn up the heat. Return the chicken to the wok and stir and turn in rapid succession for about 30 seconds, or until hot. Splash in the wine or sherry around the side of the wok, stirring continuously as it sizzles. Add the salt and sugar and sprinkle on the ground peppercorns. Trickle in the well-stirred, dissolved cornstarch and continue to stir as it thickens. Return the chilies to the wok and stir to mix for about another 10 seconds. Sprinkle on the sesame oil, then transfer to a warm serving plate. Serve immediately.

# Paper-thin Lamb with Scallions

This is one of the famous Peking dishes. The scallions are an indispensable ingredient, because they add so much flavor to the lamb, not to mention increasing the overall fragrance of the dish.

**1** Slice the lamb into paper-thin pieces (chilling the meat in the refrigerator beforehand for 1 or 2 hours to make slicing easier). Pat dry, if necessary. Put into a bowl.

**2 Prepare the marinade:** Add the soy sauce and wine or sherry to the lamb. Let marinate for 20 to 30 minutes.

**3 Prepare the sauce:** Mix together the salt, sugar, soy sauce, wine or sherry and oil in a small bowl and put aside.

**4** Heat a wok over high heat until smoke rises. Add the oil and swirl it around. Add the garlic; let it sizzle and take on color. Put in the lamb and, sliding the wok scoop or metal spatula to the bottom of the wok, turn and toss for 20 to 30 seconds, or until partially cooked. Pour in the sauce, stirring to incorporate, and add the scallions. Flip and toss until the lamb is cooked and the mixture has absorbed most of the sauce. The dish should be slightly dry in appearance.

**5** Remove to a warm serving plate and sprinkle with sesame oil to enhance the flavor. Serve immediately.

### INGREDIENTS

12 ounces (350 grams) lamb loin, trimmed
3 or 4 tablespoons peanut or corn oil
2 cloves garlic, peeled and sliced thin
8 ounces (225 grams) scallions, sliced
 into long slivers
dashes of sesame oil to taste

**For the marinade**
2 teaspoons thin soy sauce
2 teaspoons Shaohsing wine
 or medium-dry sherry

**For the sauce**
¼ teaspoon salt
½ teaspoon sugar
2 teaspoons thick soy sauce
2 teaspoons Shaohsing wine
 or medium-dry sherry
1 teaspoon sesame oil

**SERVES 4 with 2 other dishes**

# Plain-boiled Vegetables

In the South, where green vegetables grow in abundance, boiling is as popular a method of cooking as stir-frying. Chinese flowering cabbage and broccoli are especially suitable.

**1** Put 5 cups of water into a saucepan and bring to a boil. Add the salt and 1½ tablespoons of the oil.

**2** Place the cabbage in the water and return to a boil. Boil for about 30 to 60 seconds. It should be tender but still have a bite. Drain well in a colander.

**3** Transfer the cabbage to a warm serving plate. Pour the rest of the oil over it evenly and then the oyster or soy sauce. Serve hot.

### INGREDIENTS

1 teaspoon salt
4 tablespoons peanut or corn oil
1 pound (450 grams) Chinese flower
 cabbage, trimmed
2 tablespoons oyster sauce or
 1½ tablespoons soy sauce

**SERVES 6 with 3 other dishes**

# Lion's Head

## INGREDIENTS

1 pound (450 grams) Chinese celery
  cabbage
8 water chestnuts, fresh peeled or
  canned drained
1 pound (450 grams) pork,
  about 2 to 3 ounces
  (55 to 85 grams) of which is fat
scant 3 tablespoons water
½ teaspoon salt
2 tablespoons thick soy sauce
1 tablespoon Shaohsing wine
  or medium-dry sherry
1 teaspoon brown sugar
1 tablespoon cornstarch
3 tablespoons peanut or corn oil
1 cup clear stock
2 or 3 teaspoons potato flour

**SERVES 6** with 3 other dishes

This dish originated in Yangchow, in Kiangsu Province. It is so called because each pork meat cake is supposed to resemble a lion's head, and the cabbage its mane.

**1** Cut each cabbage leaf crosswise into 2-inch (5-centimeter) pieces, separating the stalk from the leafy top pieces.

**2** Chop the water chestnuts by hand or mince coarsely.

**3** Chop the pork by hand or mince coarsely. Put into a large bowl. Stir in the water, 1 tablespoon at a time, and continue to stir in the same direction for 1 or 2 minutes, or until smooth and almost gelatinous. Pick up the pork mixture and throw it back into the bowl about 20 to 30 times. This stirring and throwing action makes the pork light and tender, producing the desired effect when cooked.

**4** Add the salt, soy sauce, wine or sherry and sugar and mix well. Stir in the water chestnuts. Divide the mixture into 4 equal portions, shaping them into thick round cakes—each a lion's head.

**5** Mix the cornstarch and water into a thin paste in a slope-sided plate. Roll the lions' heads in the paste to coat all over.

**6** Heat a wok over moderate heat. Add the oil and when smoke rises, put in the lions' heads to brown, 2 at a time, for about 2 minutes each side or until golden in color. Transfer to a plate, leaving the oil in the wok.

**7** Add the stalk pieces of the cabbage and stir-fry for about 30 seconds, then add the leafy pieces and continue to stir-fry for another minute to cook partially and reduce their bulk.

**8** Transfer half of this cabbage to line the bottom of a large flameproof or ovenproof casserole. Place the lions' heads on top, then cover them with the remaining cabbage, adding the oil from the wok as well. Add the stock.

**9** To cook, either: bring the casserole to a boil on top of a stove. Lower the heat and simmer, covered, for 2 hours. This traditional way produces the best result. Or cook in a preheated oven at 350°F (180°C) for 20 minutes, reduce the heat to 325°F (160°C) and continue to cook for a further 2 hours.

**10** To serve, arrange the cabbage underneath and around the meat cakes on a warm plate, to give the illusion of a lion's head and mane. Thicken the sauce with the potato flour mixed with a little water and pour over the meat.

# Dried Oysters
# and Hair Seaweed

The Chinese are very fond of puns, and the Chinese language lends itself
particularly to play on words, for it is very rich in tones. Mandarin, the official
language, has four tones to each sound; Cantonese, the lingua franca in the
South, has at least seven. This often allows two, or even three, meanings to
a term, each with a slightly different pronunciation. This dish, beloved of the
Cantonese, is a classic example of this point. Dried oyster and hair seaweed
sounds similar to the Chinese New Year greeting: "Good deeds and prosperity"
or "Good business and prosperity." For this reason, Southern Chinese make
sure they eat this dish during the first fortnight of the Chinese New Year,
when much food and many different dishes are consumed.

**1** Rinse the dried oysters thoroughly, rubbing gently with the fingers to get rid
of any impurities. Put into a bowl and pour over them sufficient boiling water
to just cover. Soak for about 3 or 4 hours or even overnight, until quite soft.
Remove and discard the hard muscles. Reserve soaking liquid.

**2** Soak the hair seaweed in plenty of cold or tepid water for about 10 minutes,
so that it will become pliable. Then squeeze and rinse in many changes of water,
picking it over, removing impurities and discarding the fine sand that settles
at the bottom of the bowl.

**3 Cure the hair seaweed:** Put the water, ginger slices, wine or sherry and
oil in a wok and bring to a boil. Submerge the seaweed and boil for about
5 minutes. Drain through a fine sieve and discard the ginger.

**4** Drain and squeeze out excess water from the mushrooms, but leave damp.
Reserve the soaking liquid.

**5** Cut the pork belly into rectangular pieces of more or less the same size
as the dried oysters.

**6** Heat a wok over high heat until smoke rises. Add the oil and swirl it around.
Add the garlic, stir, then the ginger, stir, and the white scallions and stir. Add the
pork, oysters and mushrooms and, sliding the wok scoop or metal spatula to the
bottom of the wok, turn and toss gently for about 1 minute or until very hot. Splash
in the wine or sherry around the side of the wok. When the sizzling dies down,

## INGREDIENTS

24 dried oysters
½ ounce (15 grams) hair seaweed
16 medium dried Chinese mushrooms,
  reconstituted in 1½ cups boiling water
  (see page 33)
12 ounces (350 grams) roast pork belly
  (see page 146)
2 or 3 tablespoons peanut or corn oil
1 or 2 cloves garlic, peeled and cut
  diagonally into thin slices
4 to 6 thin slices fresh ginger root, peeled
6 scallions, white parts only, cut into
  1-inch (2.5-centimeter) sections
1 tablespoon Shaohsing wine or
  medium-dry sherry
2 cups liquid, made up of oyster water,
  mushroom water and clear stock
2 tablespoons oyster sauce
1 tablespoon thin soy sauce
½ teaspoon sugar
2 tablespoons potato flour, dissolved
  in ½ cup water

**For curing hair seaweed**

2 cups water
2 thickish slices fresh ginger root, peeled
2 teaspoons Shaohsing wine or
  medium-dry sherry
2 teaspoons peanut or corn oil

**SERVES 8** with 4 or 5 other dishes

add the liquid, oyster sauce, soy sauce and sugar. Bring to a boil, reduce the heat and simmer fast, covered, for about 30 to 45 minutes.

**7** Make a well in the middle of the wok contents, add the seaweed and continue to simmer fast for another 15 minutes. Add more liquid if necessary—at the end of the cooking time there should be about ¾ to 1 cup of liquid still unabsorbed.

**8** Leaving the liquid in the wok, remove the pork, oysters and mushrooms and arrange them attractively on a warm serving plate or in a bowl. Place the whole bunch of seaweed on top in the center so that your family or guests recognize the symbolic greeting of prosperity immediately.

**9** Return the liquid in the wok to simmering point. Mix in sufficient well-stirred dissolved potato flour to thicken the sauce enough to coat the back of a spoon. Pour over the ingredients and serve hot.

# Eight–treasure Rice Pudding

## INGREDIENTS

12 ounces (350 grams) white glutinous rice
2 cups water
6 dried Chinese red dates
2 tablespoons all-purpose flour
10 ounces (280 grams) canned red bean paste
2 tablespoons peanut or corn oil
¼ cup lard
3 tablespoons sugar
1 glacé cherry
18 small cubes candied orange peel
18 golden raisins
18 black raisins

**For the syrup**
Either:
3 tablespoons sugar
1 cup water
2 teaspoons cornstarch, dissolved in 2 tablespoons water
Or:
½ cup maple syrup

**SERVES 8**

This Northern pudding is served anytime, but more especially during Chinese New Year. "Eight-treasure" is a reference to the eight treasures in Buddhism that guard and enrich one's life. For decorating the pudding, nuts or other dried fruits can be substituted.

**1** Wash the glutinous rice 3 or 4 times, or until the water is no longer milky. Drain and put into a baking pan or a heatproof plate. Add the water. Steam in a wok or steamer for about 25 minutes (see page 43).

**2** Meanwhile, soak the dates in hot water for 15 minutes, then slit open and remove the pits, leaving the dates whole.

**3 Prepare the red bean paste:** Add the flour to the bean paste and blend well. Heat a wok or frying pan over moderate heat, add the oil and then the bean paste. Cook for about 5 minutes, turning and stirring all the time to prevent it from sticking. This thickens it sufficiently to keep it from leaking through the rice during steaming. Remove and leave to cool.

**4** Well grease a 4-cup glass heatproof bowl, with some of the lard.

**5** Blend the remaining lard and the sugar into the cooked rice.

**6** Form a decorative pattern in the bottom of the bowl with the dried fruits. Put the cherry in the center. Make a ring of 6 triangles around it with the orange peel. Make 6 lines, alternating golden and black raisins, to go up the sides of the bowl between the orange peel. Place 1 red date between the lines of raisins.

**7** Gently but *firmly* press one fairly thick layer of rice on the bottom and sides of the bowl to cover the dried fruits without disturbing the pattern. Put the red bean paste in the center. Cover with the remaining rice, pressing down to make the surface flat and even. There should be about 1 inch (2.5 centimeters) between the rice level and the rim of the bowl, so that the rice does not overflow when steamed.

**8** Put the bowl inside the wok or steamer and steam for about 1¼ hours. Check the water level periodically, adding more if necessary.

**9** About 15 minutes before the rice pudding is ready, prepare the syrup. If the traditional syrup is used, put the sugar and water in a saucepan and slowly bring to a boil. When the sugar is completely dissolved, trickle in the dissolved cornstarch, stirring as the mixture thickens. Pour into a warm bowl. Alternatively, bring the maple syrup to a boil and pour into a warm bowl. This syrup complements the pudding well, in both flavor and color.

**10** Remove the bowl from the wok or steamer and invert the pudding onto a warm plate, so that the decorative pattern is on top. The best way to do this is to put the bowl in the middle of a long towel. Cover the bowl with the plate. Pick up the towel, bowl and plate with both hands and turn upside down, then gently remove the bowl as the rice pudding slips onto the plate.

**11** Pour the syrup over it and serve hot.

# Szechwan Chili Paste

### INGREDIENTS

dried red chilies
ground yellow bean sauce

**1** Grind sufficient red chilies in a food processor or use a mortar and pestle.

**2** In a bowl, mix the chilies and the yellow bean sauce, in the proportion of 1 tablespoon ground chili to 2 tablespoons ground yellow bean sauce. (Natives of Szechwan will no doubt find this proportion too mild, and people unused to spicy foods will find it almost too hot. Use your judgment to suit your own taste.) The chili paste will keep for months in a jar stored in a cool place.

# Hot Chili Oil

### INGREDIENTS

12 dried red chilies, each about 3 inches (7.5 centimeters) long, or 24 small ones
1 cup peanut or corn oil

This is sometimes sold in a bottle as Chili oil, but I prefer the taste of this homemade version.

**1** Slit open the dried chilies. Remove and discard the seeds. Chop into flakes and put into a glass jar.

**2** Heat the oil in a saucepan until it smokes. Remove at once from the heat. Let cool for 3 or 4 minutes.

**3** Pour into the jar. The chili flakes will rise to the surface but will sink to the bottom gradually. The oil becomes spicy hot almost immediately, but will become more so in a few days time. It keeps for months in a cool place.

# Sweet Bean Sauce

## INGREDIENTS

1 tablespoon water
9 tablespoons sugar
9 tablespoons ground yellow bean sauce
1 tablespoon peanut or corn oil

**1** Put the water, sugar, yellow bean sauce and oil in a wok or saucepan. Heat over low heat for 3 or 4 minutes, or until the sugar has completely dissolved, stirring all the time to mix into a smooth sauce.

**2** Let cool and serve at room temperature.

# Flavor-potting

## INGREDIENTS FOR THE SAUCE

4 ounces (115 grams) mixed flavor-potting
  spices or 12 whole star anise
½ ounce (15 grams) cinnamon
1 cardamom (t'sao kuo)
1 teaspoon cloves
3 tablespoons fennel seeds
4 tablespoons Szechwan peppercorns
⅕ ounce (5 grams) licorice
1 ounce (25 grams) dried ginger root
10 to 11 cups water
2 ounces (55 grams) fresh ginger root,
  unpeeled and bruised
2 or 3 large pieces preserved tangerine peel
2 tablespoons sea salt
2 cups thick soy sauce
¼ cup thin soy sauce
5 ounces (140 grams) Demerara or
  granulated sugar
6 ounces (175 grams) Shaohsing wine or
  medium-dry sherry
2 tablespoons mei-kuei-lu wine or gin

Flavor-potting is a cooking technique popular in every Chinese region whereby meat, poultry or offal is cooked and then steeped in a specially prepared sauce. The idea is that the flavor of the sauce will permeate the meat, and the sauce will in turn be enriched by the taste of the meat and its fat. The spices used in the sauce vary from area to area and from cook to cook, but the ones most frequently used are: star anise, Szechwan peppercorns, fennel seeds, cinnamon, ginger and liquorice. In China, flavor-potting spices are generally bought ready-made from an herbal pharmacy, and these mixtures, labeled "mixed spices," are now exported and sold in Chinese shops. In this recipe I have also added preserved tangerine peel.

The flavor-potting sauce, if properly kept and periodically reheated, should last indefinitely. Indeed, many families pride themselves on keeping the same sauce for months, if not years!

**1** Put the mixed spices in a bag made from 3 layers of cheesecloth or muslin and tie the opening with cotton or string. Put into a large, deep stockpot.

**2** Add the water, fresh ginger and tangerine peel. Bring to a boil, reduce the heat and simmer for about 15 minutes, to release the aromatic flavors.

**3** Add the sea salt, soy sauces, sugar and wine or sherry, continuing to simmer until the sugar has completely dissolved. Check the taste of the sauce: it should be quite salty, rich and aromatic. It is now ready for other ingredients to be cooked in it.

# Stock

## INGREDIENTS

### PRIME STOCK

1½ pounds (675 grams) chicken thighs, drumsticks and necks

1½ pounds (675 grams) mostly lean pork, without rind

1½ pounds (675 grams) ham or mild gammon, without rind

**MAKES 6 CUPS**

### CLEAR STOCK

leftover ingredients from prime stock

salt to taste

**MAKES ABOUT 3½ CUPS**

There are many ways of making stock, but the Chinese believe that the most balanced result comes from a long simmering of chicken, pork and ham. Abalone was traditionally included, but because it is now so expensive, most people are content to dispense with it. In the Chinese kitchen, a distinction is made between the first yield of this simmering, called "prime stock," and the second yield, called "clear or secondary stock."

A question often raised is whether or not you should use stock cubes. If you are desperate, by all means use them, but I suggest using them only in an emergency. Stock keeps well in the refrigerator for up to a week but will keep longer if brought to a boil every second day.

### Prime Stock:

**1** Put the chicken, pork and ham or gammon into a deep stockpot or saucepan and add 10 cups of water. Bring to a boil and skim off the scum that surfaces until the water is clear.

**2** Partially cover with a lid. Lower the heat to maintain a fast simmer and cook for about 3 hours. The liquid, which should have reduced to about 6 cups, is the prime stock. Pour through a sieve into a storage container. Refrigerate.

**Note:** The meat in the stockpot is still tasty enough to serve as a meal if clear or secondary stock is not to be made. Dip the chicken or pork in thin soy sauce and eat the ham as it is.

### Clear Stock:

**1** Refill the stockpot or saucepan with 6 to 8 cups of water. Bring to a boil, reduce the heat to maintain a fast simmer and cook, partially covered, for 1½ to 2 hours, reducing the liquid to 3 to 4 cups. This is the clear or secondary stock.

**2** Pour through a sieve into a storage container. Discard the meat. Season with salt to taste. Keep in the refrigerator.

**Variation:** Another way of making prime and clear stock is to use about 4½ pounds (2 kilograms) of pork or ham bones, spare ribs, chicken or duck carcass, giblets and stalks from dried Chinese mushrooms. Simmer them in about 14 cups of water, reducing the liquid to about 9 cups for prime stock. Add water again to make more or less the same amount for clear or secondary stock.

# Vegetables

**Bamboo shoots *(Dendrocalamus latiflorus)*** The young shoots of several species of bamboo cultivated for consumption in China. Those available from November to January are called winter shoots and those available from January to April are called spring shoots. Fresh bamboo shoots are only occasionally available in the West; what are available, however, are canned bamboo shoots in chunks or in slices; they should be rinsed before use. If they are not all used at once, the remainder must be transferred to another container, covered with water and refrigerated. If the water is changed every other day, they keep well for 2 to 3 weeks.

**Bean sprouts *(Phaseolus aureus)*** Sprouts from small green mung beans, about 2 to 4 inches (7.5 to 10 centimeters) long. When choosing these sprouts, which are high in protein, look for those that are white and plump and avoid any that are limp and yellow. Although bean sprouts can be eaten raw in salads, the Chinese prefer to eat them slightly cooked but retaining their light and crisp qualities. Fresh bean sprouts can be kept refrigerated in a plastic bag for up to 3 days. Do not buy canned bean sprouts; they are just a soggy mass.

**Chinese broccoli *(Brassica alboglabra)*, Chinese kale, gaai-laan** Chinese broccoli is distinguished by its oval-shaped leaves, which have a bluish green sheen, and the white flowers in the middle of the plant. The stalk is like that

of broccoli but the taste is more pronounced, reminiscent of asparagus. It keeps in the refrigerator for about 3 days.

**Chinese cabbage *(Brassica chinensis)*, Chinese white cabbage, bok-choy, bai-tsai** Thick, white-skinned cabbage with tender dark green leaves. It is similar in appearance to Swiss chard, but it is sweeter and juicier.

**Chinese celery cabbage *(Brassica pekinensis)*, Tientsin cabbage, Peking cabbage, Chinese leaves, wong nga baak** A tight head of cylindrical white stalks extending into yellowish-white crinkled leaves. This Northern Chinese vegetable is popular among most Chinese because of its sweet, mild flavor and its versatility: it can be stir-fried, braised and put into soups. In recent years, it has become popular in the West and is therefore available in supermarkets. Choose firm heads and see that the leaves are not shriveled. If refrigerated, it keeps for about 2 to 3 weeks.

**Chinese chives *(Allium tuberosum)*** Similar to chives in appearance, they are, however, darker green in color, more fibrous in texture, stronger in taste and have flat, not tubular, leaves. They are available only in Chinese supermarkets and keep well in a plastic bag in the refrigerator.

**Chinese flowering cabbage *(Brassica parachinensis)*, choi-sum** This vegetable is distinguished by its yellow flowers and

long stems of about 6 to 8 inches (15 to 20 centimeters). It has a subtle taste, and is a great favorite of the Southern Chinese, served either stir-fried or simply blanched; the stems need not be peeled. It keeps well in the refrigerator for about 3 days.

**Ginkgo nuts *(Ginkgo biloba)*, silver apricot** The ginkgo tree was originally a sacred Chinese tree, but it now grows in Japan and other parts of the world. The nuts, pits of the ginkgo fruit, have to be cracked and peeled. Unfortunately, the flesh inside the beige shell seems to dry up easily, with the result that exported nuts are often rotten and hard inside. It is therefore advisable to use canned gingko nuts. Mild and tender, they are a favorite of vegetarians. Any leftover nuts should be transferred to a container, covered with water and put in the refrigerator.

**Hair seaweed *(Borgia fuscopurpurea)*, cow hair seaweed, fa-t'sai** Black, hairlike moss, this product of the Hopeh and Shensi provinces is sold in a dried form and must be reconstituted by soaking. Totally tasteless alone, it absorbs other flavors and provides a slippery and bouncy texture. Stored in a covered container, it keeps indefinitely.

**Mustard green *(Brassica juncea)*, mustard cabbage, gaai-choi** There are many varieties of mustard green and some, with their bitter tangy taste, are more suitable for pickling than cooking.

A common variety, whose green stalks extend into single, large oval, ribbed leaves, has a distinctive taste when simply blanched or put into soup. It is only sold in Chinese supermarkets. Choose firm green plants and avoid those with limp yellow leaves. It keeps well for a few days in a plastic bag in the refrigerator.

**Red-in-snow** *(Brassica juncea var. multiceps)*, **pickled cabbage** A red-rooted variety of mustard plant grown in Chekiang province which, being very resistant to cold, can be seen sprouting up through the spring snows, hence the name. This crisp green vegetable is cut and preserved in salt. Available in cans and soaked in brine, it is mostly used as an accompaniment to pork or in soup.

**Sugar peas, snow peas, mange tout** *(Pisum sativum)* Tender green peapods containing flat, barely formed peas. Valued for their crisp texture and sweet, subtle flavor, they are best stir-fried. When choosing, look for the flat, tender green ones. If refrigerated in a plastic bag, they will keep for more than 1 week.

**Szechwan preserved vegetable** *(Brassica juncea var. tsatsai)*, **cha-t'sai, ja-choi** Made from the swollen nodules on the stems of a species of mustard plant grown in Szechwan province, which have been preserved in salt, pressed to squeeze out much of their liquid content and then pickled with a fine red chili powder. The chili has to be rinsed off before use. Spicy hot and salty, it gives both a crisp texture and a peppery flavor to other ingredients. Sold in cans, it keeps for a long time if stored in a covered jar.

**Taro** *(Colocasia antiquorum)* Root vegetable that, whether small, like potatoes, or long and fat like yams, has dark brown skin, often with earth-encrusted root hairs, and a gray or purple flesh. When choosing, press the skin to make sure that it is firm, rather than soft, rotten or dried up. When cooked, it is slimy. It is often cooked with duck or fatty pork. Taro keeps well in a cool place for more than a week.

**Water chestnuts** *(Eleocharis tuberosa)* Fresh water chestnuts are the walnut-sized bulbs of a sedge cultivated in swampy paddy fields or in muddy ponds. As a result,

their mahogany-colored skin is often encrusted with mud, but when washed and peeled, the flesh is white, very crisp and subtly sweet; they can be eaten raw. Canned water chestnuts, although less crisp and sweet, will provide a crunchy texture to vegetables and meat dishes. Press fresh water chestnuts to make sure they are not rotten or dried up. They can be kept in the refrigerator for up to a week. Canned ones last up to 1 week if covered with water.

**Winter melon** *(Benincasa hispida)* Wax gourd with a white pulp, it can weigh from a few pounds up to 100 pounds (45 kilograms); it is often cut up and sold by weight in wedges. When buying a wedge, make sure that the pulp has not dried up or turned yellow. The flesh, which when cooked is almost transparent, is often used in soup with pork, chicken or duck. A whole winter melon keeps for 2 to 3 months in a cool place; a wedge keeps for up to a week if refrigerated in a plastic bag.

**Young corn** *(Zea mays)* Tender, miniature corn on the cob, usually sold in cans. They are either put into vegetarian dishes or used as an ingredient with meat.

# Herbs and Spices

**Cassia** *(Cinnamomum cassia)*, **Chinese cinnamon** Dried bark of the cassia tree. It is used in the master sauce for flavor-potting and is one of the ingredients of five-spice powder. Cinnamon sticks can be used as an alternative.

**Dried red chilies** *(Capsicum frutescens)*, **chili peppers** Crimson red, often simply called dried chilies, they are sold in two sizes: small, up to 1¹/₂ inches (3.5 centimeters) long and large, about 3

inches (7.5 centimeters) or longer. An indispensable ingredient in Szechwan/Hunan cuisine, they provide fiery spiciness. For the uninitiated, it is perhaps advisable to remove the seeds and the white internal walls, since they are the hottest part of a chili. They keep indefinitely in a covered container.

**Coriander** *(Coriandrum sativum)*, **Chinese parsley, cilantro** Fresh, green herb with a long stalk branching into flat, serrated leaves; usually sold by the bunch.

Pungent, acidic and aromatic, it is used both as a garnish and as a seasoning, especially in Northern China. It will remain fresh for up to a week if refrigerated in an open plastic bag.

**Five-spice powder** Golden brown powder, consisting of five and sometimes six ground spices, with a licorice-like flavor. The four basic spices are: star anise, cassia or Chinese cinnamon, cloves and fennel seeds. The remainder are often

Szechwan peppercorns and sometimes ginger and cardamom. Five-spice powder is mostly used in marinades for meat, poultry or fish, but it must be used sparingly. It is sold in small packages and can be kept indefinitely in a covered jar.

**Flavor-potting mixed spices** Labeled Mixed Spices, these ready-mixed packages are sold in Chinese stores especially for use in flavor-potting. Each packet contains the most commonly used spices in flavor-potting: star anise, Szechwan peppercorns (fagara), cinnamon, ginger, fennel seeds, cloves, licorice and cardamom.

**Garlic (Allium sativum)** The bulb of a perennial plant. Like ginger root and scallions, it is indispensable in Chinese cooking.

**Ginger powder** Dried ginger root ground into a powder. Used as a seasoning, it cannot be used as a substitute for fresh ginger root.

**Ginger root, fresh (Zingiber officinale)** The knobbly, yellowish green root stalk of the ginger plant. Spicy hot in taste, it is used to provide flavor and to counter rank odor, especially fishiness. Like garlic and scallions, it is an essential ingredient in Chinese cooking, dating back to the Han times. Choose firm ginger with smooth skin. It keeps well if refrigerated in a perforated plastic bag.

**Ground roasted Szechwan peppercorns** Szechwan peppercorns roasted in a dry wok and then ground up into a powder. Used to add aroma to other ingredients, they can be made at home.

**Scallions (Allium cepa), spring onions** A young onion with a long, white bulb topped with tubular green leaves. "White" refers to the firm, essentially white, section which makes up most of the onion; "green" refers to the leaves. The roots attached to the white end must be chopped off and discarded before use. Dating back to the Han times, scallions form one of the three basic condiments in Chinese cooking; the other two are garlic and ginger. They keep fresh in the refrigerator for a few days.

**Shallots (Allium ascalonicum)** Small, firm onions with a milder flavor than Spanish onions.

**Star anise (Illicium verum)** Shaped like a star, with eight segments, and reddish brown in color, this hard spice is widely used in Chinese cooking to flavor meat and poultry; it has a distinctive liquorice taste and aroma. It keeps indefinitely in a covered jar.

**Szechwan peppercorns (Xanthoxylum piperitum)** Tiny, reddish-brown peppercorns which have a stronger aroma than black peppercorns and produce a numbing rather than a burning effect. Available both whole and seeded. The seeded variety has a better aroma and flavor.

**White sesame seeds (Sesamum indicum)** Tiny, flat seeds from the sesame plant; they keep for a long time in a covered container. (See also sesame oil and sesame paste.)

# Cereals, Grains and Noodles

**Buckwheat noodles** Very thin, beige-colored noodle strips made of buckwheat flour and wheat flour with water. They are a great favorite of the Northern Chinese and are available as dry noodles in some Chinese and Japanese stores.

**Cellophane noodles, transparent vermicelli, bean thread** Made from ground mung beans, these noodles are usually sold in a bundle tied by a thin thread. Wiry and hard in their dry state, they have to be soaked in water and then drained before use. Not so much as a staple, they are eaten as a vegetable, which absorbs tastes from other ingredients and provides a slippery texture. They keep indefinitely in a cool place.

**Egg noodles, fresh or dry** Made of wheat flour, egg and water, these are the most common all-purpose Chinese noodles. They are usually sold in two widths: thin thread-like and broad strip. Fresh, soft noodles are sold in plastic bags; dry noodles are sold in compressed rounds (often called noodle cakes) and are sometimes precooked by steaming. Fresh noodle cakes keep well in a sealed bag in the refrigerator for up to a week or they can be frozen if each is wrapped individually. Dried noodles keep for months in a covered jar. Egg noodles, seldom made at home, are bought in Chinese grocery stores. Noodles from other countries can be used as a substitute; the only difference is that Chinese noodles are more elastic in texture.

**Long-grain rice (Oryza sativa, spp.)** The white grains of this versatile rice are husked and polished. It is known that the Chinese grew and ate this rice as early as the 12th century BC in the Chou dynasty, and indeed, it remains the staple food for the Chinese today. Rice keeps for months in a covered container.

**Rice noodles, rice sticks** Wiry white noodles made from rice flour. Although slender too, they do not look translucent, like cellophane noodles. They are sold, dried, in tightly folded bundles and keep for months in a covered jar. Only a brief soaking and cooking time are required.

**River rice noodles** Made from rice ground with water, steamed in thin sheets, then rolled and cut up into strips about ½ inch (1 centimeter) wide, these are sold both dry and fresh. The dry noodles have to be boiled and drained before use. Despite the fact that the dry variety will last for months in a covered jar, the fresh ones are by far superior, especially for stir-frying. However, they must be used within 1 or 2 days after buying or they will lose their tender quality.

**Spring roll wrappers** Two types: Cantonese, which are smooth, like noodle dough, and Shanghai, which are transparent, like rice paper. Sold frozen, they are easily pulled apart when defrosted. The Shanghai type is used in this book.

**Tientsin fen pi** Dry, transparent, brittle round sheets, about 9 inches (23 centimeters) in diameter, made from ground mung beans. When soaked in boiling water, they have a slippery texture and are eaten as a cross between rice noodles and cellophane noodles. They keep for a long time in a cool place.

**U-dong noodles** Off-white noodle strips about ⅛ inch (2 millimeters) wide, made of wheat flour and water. These Japanese and Korean noodles are similar in texture to Northern Chinese noodles and are available as dry noodles in Oriental stores.

**White glutinous rice** *(Oryza sativa spp.)* More rounded in shape than long-grain rice, white glutinous rice is sticky when boiled. It is eaten by the Chinese both as a savory dish (see Stir-fried glutinous rice) and as a pudding (see Eight-treasure rice pudding); it is also used as a stuffing (see Duck stuffed with glutinous rice). It keeps for months in a covered container.

**Wonton wrappers** Made of the same dough as egg noodles (wheat flour, egg and water), and sold in 3 inch (7.5 centimeter) squares. They are not usually made at home but are bought fresh from Chinese stores. They can be frozen.

**Yi noodles, yifu noodles** Egg noodles woven into a round cake, already deep-fried when sold in Chinese stores. They keep well in a cool place for about 2 weeks. If left too long, they may become rancid.

# Dried Products

**Abalone** *(Haliotis tuberculata)* For most people, this shelled mollusk is available only in canned form, with its ivory-colored flesh already cooked. Even so, it is delicious eaten cold or hot, alone or with other ingredients. If eaten hot, it must be cooked very briefly; overcooking will make it rubbery. The juice in the can is valuable as a basis for sauces or soups.

**Agar** Processed gelatin extracted from dried seaweed, it is usually sold in bundles of long, narrow crinkly strips. Used as a thickener, it is extremely heat resistant and can only be dissolved slowly in boiling water. Store in a sealed plastic bag in a cool place, but *not* in the refrigerator.

**Bird's nest** Nests made by swallows of the genus Collocalia, which live on the cliffs of the Southeast Asian islands. What makes these nests unique is that the birds line them with a gelatinous mixture of predigested seaweed, which hardens to form a transparent layer. There are many grades of bird's nest, but since whole nests are extremely expensive and rarely available in the West, it is all right to use the broken ones. The whiter the color and the fewer specks of feathers there are, the better the quality of the nest. Sold in Chinese stores, they are usually preprocessed, so the cleaning job is not too laborious.

**Chinese black mushrooms** *(Lentinus edodes)* Edible tree fungi that add both flavor and texture to a dish. They vary in

quality, size and price. The best and most expensive are the floral mushrooms (*fa gu* in Cantonese, *hua ku* in Mandarin). These have floral patterns on the surface of the caps, which curl under. Second in quality are the mushrooms whose relatively thick caps also curl slightly inward along the edges. The lowest quality are the mushrooms that have thin flat caps. Usually available in Chinese stores are packages of mixed quality and sizes. They keep for a long time in a covered container.

**Chinese sausages** Wind-dried pork, or pork and duck-liver sausages, usually sold in pairs about 6 inches (15 centimeters) long. The pork sausages should look pinkish with white pork fat showing through the casing; the liver sausages should look dark brown. Both types must be cooked before eating. In a covered jar, they will keep for months in the refrigerator.

**Cloud ears** *(Auricularia auricula)*
Edible tree fungi grown in large quantities in the western provinces of Szechwan, Hunan and Yunnan. Thin and brittle when dry, they expand to form thick brown clusters when soaked for about twenty minutes. More delicate and refined than wood ears, they are used in stir-fried dishes to absorb flavors from other seasonings and, above all, to provide a slimy but crunchy texture. They should be well rinsed to remove sand, and the hard knobs should be removed if necessary. Store in a covered container.

**Cornstarch** Fine, white starch extracted from corn, it is used to thicken sauces and marinades.

**Creamed coconut** Milky white in color and solid in form, like a bar of soap, concentrated coconut milk can be kept in the refrigerator for months.

**Dried red dates** *(Ziziphus jujuba)*
Dried red fruits of the jujube tree. They have a sweet, prunelike taste.

**Edible jellyfish** *(Rhopilema esculenta)*
Beige in color and rubbery, this jellyfish is sold in round sheets about 15 to 16 inches (38 to 40 centimeters) in diameter, dried, folded and packaged in a plastic bag with large grains of salt between the folds. The salt must be shaken off and the jellyfish soaked in water for 2 to 3 days before use. Jellyfish already cut up in strips is also available, but less economical to buy. Jellyfish keep indefinitely in a sealed bag.

**Golden needles** *(Hemerocallis fulva),* **tiger-lily buds** Dried buds of the tiger-lily flower, which grows in abundance in Northern China. Usually about 3 inches (7.5 centimeters) long, they are called golden needles because of their color and shape. They absorb the tastes of other ingredients that they are cooked with and also provide a subtle lightness of texture. They keep indefinitely if stored in a covered jar or in a sealed plastic bag.

**Oysters** *(Crassostrea gigas)* Brown, rectangular and quite firm to the touch, these oysters have been salted and dried in the sun. Considered an epicurean delicacy, they add a "smoky" taste to meat and bland ingredients. Because they are expensive, make sure that they are not moldy when you buy them. If refrigerated they keep for a long time.

**Potato flour** Flour ground from cooked potatoes. As a thickening agent, it is more gelatinous than cornstarch and gives a more subtle and glossy finish to a sauce. In thickening the same amount of liquid, use about two-thirds the amount of potato flour as you would cornstarch. Tapioca and arrowroot are also popular thickening agents.

**Rock sugar, crystal sugar** This crystallized, pale topaz-colored cane sugar comes in lumps and has a "pure" taste. Demerara sugar comes closest to it in taste but white granulated sugar can also be used as a substitute. It keeps indefinitely in a dry container.

**Scallops** *(Amusium pleuronectes)*
Golden and round, the large ones weighing between ⅓ to ½ ounce (8 to 15 grams) each, these are white scallops that have been dried in the sun. Inherently sweet, they are used to add a sweet flavor to

other ingredients; they are also used as the main ingredient in sophisticated dishes such as Dried scallop soup (see page 67). They keep for a long time in a covered jar in a cool place.

**Shark's fin** The cured and sun-dried fin of one of several species of shark. Many countries in Asia, Europe and South America produce shark's fin, but the product from Manila, the "Manila yellow," is the best. Such fins are, however, extremely expensive and take about four days to prepare. The fin used in this book had already been processed, partially cooked and dried again, and it consisted of the cartilage with some "fin needles." Shark's fin has no taste, but when combined with other ingredients in a prime stock, it is without peer. The Chinese regard the highly nutritious shark's fin, whether in a soup or a red-braised dish, as the pinnacle of gastronomy. Store in a covered jar in a cool place.

**Shrimp** Small, shelled shrimp of various sizes, salted and dried in the sun. They are used as a seasoning for vegetables and meat and are very often used in stuffings. Choose those with a fresh, pinkish color. To store, put in a covered jar in a cool place.

**Straw mushrooms** *(Volvariella volvacea),* **paddy-straw mushrooms** Small mushrooms with cone-shaped black caps, cultivated on rice straw in paddy fields. The canned product, mostly from Taiwan, is popular but should be drained and rinsed before use. They add texture more than taste to other ingredients. (Dried straw mushrooms, with their stronger smell, are used to lend taste to bland vegetables or in soups.) Store in the refrigerator.

**Tangerine peel** Dark brown, hard and brittle dried peel of tangerines, often used in combination with star anise and Szechwan peppercorns. Sold in packages, it keeps indefinitely in a cool place.

**Water chestnut flour** Flour with a grayish tinge, ground from water chestnuts, used as a thickener in certain savory and sweet dishes when a light and subtle effect is called for.

**Wood ears (*Auricularia polytricha*)** Like cloud ears, these edible fungi are

cultivated in large quantities in Western China. They are larger in size than cloud ears, coarser in texture, often black on the surface and white underneath, and need to be cooked for a longer period of time. They are used more in soups than in stir-fried dishes. Store in a covered container.

# Beans and Bean Products

**Bean curd "cheese," red fermented** Brick red in color, very strong and cheesy in taste, this type of bean curd is fermented with salt, red rice and rice wine. It is used for flavoring meat, poultry and vegetarian dishes and is usually stored in jars or earthenware pots in 1- to 2-inch (2.5- to 5-centimeter) square cakes. After a jar has been opened, the bean curd "cheese" keeps for months if refrigerated.

**Bean curd "cheese," white fermented** Ivory in color, sold in 1-inch (2.5-centimeter) cakes, this fermented bean curd often has chili added to it. It is used to flavor certain vegetables, or is served as a side dish with rice or congee. It is sold in jars and keeps for months if refrigerated.

**Bean curd, fresh** White, custardlike product made from ground soybeans and used extensively in Chinese cooking—its role is equivalent to that of dairy products in Western cuisine. Bean curd is made from soybeans which have been finely ground with water, then strained through a cloth. The resulting "milk" is brought to a boil before gypsum is added to set it into a curd. The curd is then put into boxes and weights are applied to squeeze out the remaining whey. Because it is impractical to make at home, bean curd is usually sold in Chinese stores in cakes about 1 inch

(2.5 centimeters) thick and 2½ inches (6 centimeters) square. Bean curd keeps for up to 3 days in the refrigerator if the water in which it stands is changed every day.

**Bean curd, puffed** Fresh bean curd cubes, deep-fried until golden in color and airy inside. They keep well in the refrigerator for about a week.

**Bean curd sheets** Thin, dried bean curd sheets, about 6 by 18 inches (15 to 46 centimeters), sold with about one-third of their length folded in. To make them pliable, either soak them or spray them with water. Store them in a cool, dry place.

**Black beans, fermented** Whole soybeans preserved in salt and ginger. Although pungent in taste, when combined with garlic and cooked in oil they lend a delicious flavor to any other ingredients. Some black beans are canned in brine, but the dried ones are by far the best. They keep for months if stored in a cool, dry place.

**Crushed (ground) yellow bean sauce** Nut brown purée of fermented yellow soybeans, wheat flour, salt and water. Usually sold in cans labeled "Crushed yellow bean sauce" or "Ground yellow bean sauce," this is a major seasoning in Chinese cooking of all regions.

Once opened, store in a covered jar in the refrigerator.

**Red beans (*Phaseolus angularis*), azuki beans** Native to China, but now also grown in America and Europe, these small red beans are the seeds of the plant *vigna angularis*. In Chinese cuisine they are eaten mostly as a dessert.

**Red bean paste** Thick, reddish-brown paste made from puréed, sweetened red beans or azuki beans; a very popular filling for sweet dishes.

**Soybean paste, hot** Very hot and spicy paste of soybeans crushed with chili, sugar and salt; an indispensable ingredient for making the Szechwan twice-cooked pork (see p.127). Usually sold in jars, it keeps for a long time.

**Sweet bean sauce** Made of crushed yellow bean sauce sweetened with sugar. This is the traditional dipping sauce for the famous Peking duck, although the readily available hoisin sauce is more widely used in the West.

**Szechwan chili paste, chili paste** Hot paste of dried red chili peppers and ground yellow bean sauce. It forms the basis of the famous Szechwan fish fragrant sauce. When topped with a little oil to prevent it from drying out and stored in a covered jar, it keeps for months in a cool place.

# Sauces

**Chili sauce** This tangy, orange-red sauce is made of crushed fresh chili peppers, vinegar, salt and plums. It is used both as a spicy hot seasoning and as a dip for crisp food. Store in a cool place.

**Fish sauce** Golden brown, transparent sauce made from fish, salt and water. It adds more fragrance and taste to other ingredients or sauces than a sniff of it alone might suggest. Stored in a cool place, it keeps for a long, long time.

**Hoisin sauce** Reddish brown and thick, sweet yet slightly hot, this sauce is made from soybeans, wheat flour, salt, sugar, vinegar, garlic, chili and sesame oil. It is used as a dip as well as in cooking and marinating. It keeps in a covered jar for a long time and, if refrigerated, will keep indefinitely.

**Oyster sauce** Nut brown in color, this sauce is made from oyster juice, wheat flour, cornstarch and glutinous rice, salt and sugar. Not as strong as soy sauce, the sweet and "meaty" taste it lends to other

**Yellow beans in salted sauce** Whole yellow soybeans fermented with salt, wheat flour and sugar. Although not as widely used as fermented black beans, they too are used as a seasoning when cooking meat or vegetables. Sold in cans, they should be refrigerated in a covered jar once opened.

ingredients, whether as part of a sauce mixture or as a dip for meat, poultry and vegetables, makes it a special favorite with the Cantonese. Bottled oyster sauce can be kept in a cool place; canned oyster sauce, once opened, should be transferred to a covered jar or bottle.

**Sesame sauce, sesame paste** Thick, aromatic paste of pulverized sesame seeds. The paste has to be thoroughly incorporated with the oil covering it and then thinned with oil or water before use. Tahini paste should *not* be used as a substitute; rather, use peanut butter, which has a similar fragrance.

**Shrimp paste, shrimp sauce** Made from ground shrimp fermented in brine, this paste is available in two forms: a pinkish purée and a more solid, slightly saltier paté. The purée form is used in this book. Both kinds have to be diluted with water before being used, very often to enhance the taste of bland seafood, such as squid. Usually sold in a jar, it keeps almost indefinitely in a cool place.

**Soy sauce** Made from fermented soybeans with wheat or barley, salt, sugar and yeast, this sauce is one of the most ancient seasonings in Chinese cookery. It is at once the most basic and the most versatile condiment for all Chinese cuisines, whatever the regional differences. There are two main kinds of soy sauce: the thick, also called dark, and the thin, also called light. Both are used in general cooking, for marinating and as dips. Very often they are used together with salt. It is the mark of a good cook to know how much of each to use, thereby achieving the delicious end result.

**Thick soy sauce** is thicker in consistency than thin soy sauce, darker brown in color and sweeter in taste. Since it gives a reddish brown hue to food, it is the predominant sauce in red-braised dishes and in flavor-potting. Because of its sweetness, it is preferred by many as a dip at the table.

**Thin soy sauce** is thinner in consistency, lighter brown in color and saltier in taste.

# Oils and Fats

**Chicken fat** Rendered by slowly frying the solid fat removed from near the tail and other parts of the chicken, it is used by the Chinese for stir-frying certain vegetables to enhance their flavor.

**Corn oil** Light, odorless, polyunsaturated oil processed from corn. Even though it lacks the special nutty flavor of peanut oil, it is a very satisfactory substitute because it is less expensive and more easily available.

**Hot chili oil, chili pepper oil** Easily made by steeping dried red chili flakes in hot oil (see p.240), this oil is used to add extra spiciness to food. It can be bought in bottles but the homemade product is generally superior.

**Lard** Fat rendered from pork, this used to be considered the aristocratic fat for cooking in China because of the flavor and richness it added to food. Even today cookbooks published in China call for the use of lard in stir-frying and deep-frying. However, lard is heavy and high in saturated fats, and most Chinese people do not use it for daily home cooking; they use peanut oil, corn oil or other vegetable oils instead. Lard keeps well in the refrigerator for several months.

**Peanut oil, groundnut oil** Before the introduction of peanuts or groundnuts to China from America in the 16th century, vegetable oils, in particular rapeseed oil, were commonly used for cooking. Since the intensive cultivation of peanuts in succeeding centuries, peanut oil, with its rich and nutty flavor, has become the most important cooking oil in China. Corn oil, which is much more easily available and less expensive in other parts of the world, can be used as a satisfactory substitute. (For deep-frying, however, other vegetable oils will do equally well.)

**Sesame oil, sesame seed oil** Thick, aromatic, and light brown in color, this oil is pressed from roasted white sesame seeds. As such, it is quite different from the cold-pressed Middle Eastern sesame oil, which should not be used as a substitute. Chinese sesame oil is not used for general cooking; rather, because of its heavenly aroma, it is used for marinating ingredients or for sprinkling on food just before it is served. It will keep indefinitely in a cool place.

# Wines and Vinegars

**Chinkiang vinegar** Thick, dark brown product of Chinkiang in Chekiang province, this has a low vinegar content and a special fragrance and flavor. It is used in cooking or as a dip. It comes in bottles and keeps indefinitely in a cool place. If red wine vinegar is used as a substitute, either use less of it or add more sugar.

**Kao-liang liqueur** A clear spirit made from sorghum (*kao-liang* in Chinese) grown in Northeast China. This very strong liqueur, which the Chinese drink with food, is produced in the distillery founded in Harbin in 1930. Vodka can be used as a substitute.

**Mei-kuei-lu wine** Made from Kao-liang spirit and the petals of a special species of rose, this is a very strong liqueur with a unique aroma. It is used in the master sauce for flavor-potting, and is used to add fragrance to marinades. Gin or vodka can be used as a substitute.

**Moutai wine** Production of this spirit began in 1704 in a small town called Moutai in Kweichow province, Western China. Made from wheat and sorghum, it is as much these ingredients as the local spring water that give this spirit its distinctive bouquet. It is drunk in small quantities with food.

**Red vinegar** Red in color, this vinegar is also low in vinegar content. It is usually used as a dip to go with fried noodles or Shark's fin soup because the Chinese believe that it makes these foods more easily digestable.

**Rice vinegar** Clear in color and used in cooking or pickling vegetables, this vinegar is neither as sharp nor as pungent as malt vinegar; it keeps indefinitely. Use cider or white wine vinegar as a substitute.

**Shaohsing wine** Named after the town in the eastern province of Chekiang, this yellow wine, with its golden sheen, is one of the oldest wines ever produced in China. Fermented from glutinous rice with yeast, this wine owes its fame as much to these ingredients as to the water from the Chien Lake. Between 15 and 20 proof, there are numerous brands of Shaohsing wine, differing in age and quality, although the one most commonly available in Chinese stores abroad is labeled simply Shaohsing wine. The Chinese drink it warm, with food, because it tastes much better that way. It is also used in small quantities in marinades and in cooking, to enhance the flavor and the taste of the food. Medium-dry sherry can be used as a substitute.

# Index

Page numbers in *italic* refer to the illustrations.

## ACKNOWLEDGMENTS

For their help on the 2006 edition of this book, Dorling Kindersley would like to thank the home economists Eliza Baird, Angela Boggiano and Linda Tubby; Helen Trent for her work on styling the new photography, Paul Banville for his illustration and Alamy and Dennis Cox for their kind permission to reproduce the image on page 8.

Dorling Kindersley would also like to thank those who worked on the original edition of this book: the editor Fiona MacIntyre, the art editor Sue Storey and the managing editor Amy Carroll. Thanks also go to Barbara Croxford for initial work on the recipes; Chiang Yu-ling and Charlene Stolper for assisting Yan-kit in photographic sessions; Chiang Hsueh-lien and Kuo Kang Chen for their art services; the stylist Penny Markham and Paul Williams for photography.

I would like to thank the following for encouraging and helping me embark on cookery professionally: Joanna Collingwood-Anstey, Felicity Bryan, Pamela Harlech, Nancy Royal, Alice Tessier and Caroline Waldegrave. Thanks are also due to those who have contributed ideas and materials, and to those with whom I have discussed various aspects of the book: Alan Davidson, Hilda Ho, Catherine Hwang, Kester Kong, May Kong, Charlene Stolper, So Yan-lap, Agnes Tang, Chef Lam Yi-ling and Chef Woo Kwun. I am especially grateful to Chiang Yu-ling for sharing with me her knowledge and skill on Peking and Szechwan cooking. Last, but not least, I wish to thank the editors, Barbara Crawford and Fiona MacIntyre, and the designer, Sue Storey, for their editorial and artistic effort in shaping the book.

Yan-kit So
1984

## THE AUTHOR

Yan-kit So (1933–2001) was a well-known Chinese cookery expert who successfully demonstrated her special techniques and recipes at leading London Cookery schools, including Leith's School of Food and Wine. Born in Chungshan, China, raised and educated in Hong Kong, and later in London, Yan-kit spent some time in India and the USA, but for most of her life lived in London.

Yan-kit So is the author of numerous books and articles on Chinese cuisine and she contributed recipes and features on regional cooking to *Robert Carrier's Kitchen*. She held a PhD in history from the University of London and translated several Chinese short stories for publication by the Chinese University of Hong Kong.